This Book Belongs
to
Miss Mabel Dahlquist
Southdale Nursing Home
3712 Tower Avenue
Superior, Wis. 54880
Room 4.

MY
YOUNG LIFE

MY YOUNG LIFE

BY SHIRLEY TEMPLE
AND THE EDITORS OF LOOK

GARDEN CITY PUBLISHING CO., INC.
GARDEN CITY, NEW YORK

Contents

I am grateful to numerous screen co-workers, teachers and friends for their helpful assistance in recalling early incidents and associations recounted in this book. I also wish particularly to thank the editors of LOOK Magazine, who not only suggested that I write this book but carefully researched thousands of pictures to select and write captions for those printed herein. And above all, I am indebted to my mother, without whose encouragement I should never have finished so large a task.

SHIRLEY TEMPLE

SANTA MONICA, CALIFORNIA

Preface

She is one of the best-known persons in the world.

In Bali, 20,000 people gathered on her seventh birthday and prayed for her health. In Japan, a movie magazine filled two issues solely with photographs of her, without a word of text, and sold a million copies of each. In Hawaii, 40,000 pairs of hands applauded when she stood on Princess Liliuokalani's Palace *lanais* and sang "The Good Ship Lollipop" four times—to the north, south, east and west. Her fan clubs throughout the world, at one time, had a combined membership of nearly four million adults and children. She was Captain of the Texas Rangers, Mascot of the Chilean Navy, and a Kentucky Colonel.

On her eighth birthday, she received 135,000 gifts and greetings. On her ninth birthday, Henry Morgenthau gave her a typewriter with her name on it. When she wore a hair bow in one picture, the ribbon industry boomed. Twelve thousand of her photographs were sent out each month in answer to requests from abroad.

Between her fifth and twelfth years she earned well over two million dollars.

Now, at 17, she begins a new career in entirely different roles. Looking back, Shirley Temple tells the story of the most fabulous years any little girl ever experienced.

9

Vacationing in Honolulu, Shirley was cheered by thousands as she rode through the streets with her parents in a flower-laden open car. Hawaiian children of all races imitated Shirley's simple dresses, wore their hair in a multitude of dandelion curls like hers.

The world's great were Shirley's friends. She corresponded with President Franklin Roosevelt, visited the White House (upper right), welcomed Eleanor Roosevelt to the Fox studio (lower left), and was made an honorary G-woman by J. Edgar Hoover.

Shirley Temple dresses, and Shirley Temple dolls costumed in miniature replicas of the dresses, sold by the millions, brought in royalty revenues which more than equalled Shirley's movie salary.

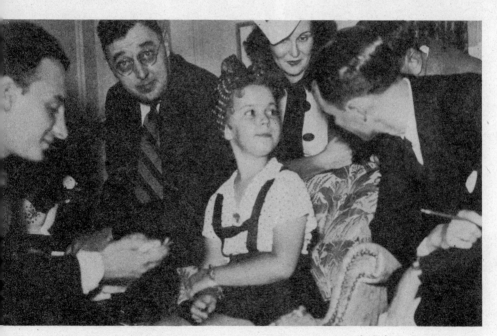

When Shirley and her parents took a cross-country motor trip, she was besieged by reporters and photographers in every city. In Boston, where this picture of a press conference was taken, newspapers ran banner headlines when she was confined to her room for three

days with a slight stomach upset. When she recovered, a crowd of five thousand gathered to watch her ride the swan boats in the public gardens. In 1939, she rode on the royal float and acted as Grand Marshal of Pasadena's famous Tournament of Roses.

At the première of *Wee Willie Winkie*, policemen held back the
mobs who pressed against ropes for a glimpse of Shirley. Often
crowds broke into spontaneous applause when Shirley appeared.

When *Stowaway* came to New York, crowds eager to see Shirley on the screen stretched for several blocks before the doors opened.

Shirley's picture has appeared at least once on the covers of dozens of national magazines. When she was a child, an average of 20 photographs of her appeared each day in magazines and newspapers.

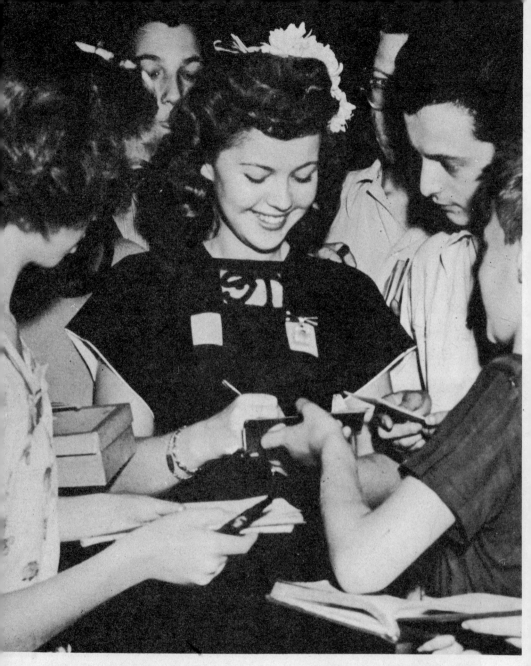

In New York City, where these young autograph hounds waited outside Shirley's hotel, her signature can be traded for two autographs of Frank Sinatra. Shirley estimates that she has responded to some 50,000 requests for autographs since the beginning of her movie career. As a child star, all her free time was regularly set aside each Friday to answer fan requests for autographed photographs.

This giant four-engined Army transport was named in Shirley's honor and christened by her. Servicemen send in a large percentage of Shirley's fan mail, which in 1944 reached a total of 185,685 letters, a sum exceeded only by Bing Crosby's. During the first three months of 1945, Shirley received 70,000 letters, which indicates that her fan mail for the year will probably reach 300,000.

This was the era into which Shirley Temple was born. Women's waistlines crept up to normal as speak-easies closed and breadlines opened. Americans played miniature golf while Hitler rode into power. Coolidge chose not to run and Hoover succeeded to the Presidency in a nation whose banks were soon to close.

Introduction

On April 23, 1928, George Temple was passing out cigars in a Los Angeles branch of the California Bank where he worked as manager. His wife, Gertrude, had just given birth to a daughter, a healthy 6½-pound child. She was born when her two brothers were 8 and 12 and was to be called Shirley Jane, because her mother liked the name.

The Temples' modest middle-class home was like thousands of others. There was a back yard where Gertrude Temple grew flowers and hung out her Monday washing. In the living room was an early radio set and a crank-winding phonograph with albums of classical recordings. Included in the record cabinet were such late hits as "I Can't Give You Anything But Love, Baby" and "Button Up Your Overcoat." In the garage stood a Paige sedan. For Shirley, there were the bassinet, baby carriage and play pen.

The Temples wore the fashions of the time. Gertrude Temple had straight, shapeless dresses with the waistline at the hips, loose coats which she held together, and round, tight helmet hats. Her evening gowns, short and low-necked, had tulle pompons on the shoulders.

Some months after Shirley's birth, Herbert Hoover was elected to succeed Calvin Coolidge. The Temples voted for him in a landslide which swept 40 states. Newspaper editorials predicted genially that the boom in stocks was sound and would continue, and George Temple came home with stories of how the office boy and the cleaning woman had made their fortunes by buying stocks on margin.

Over their morning coffee, the Temples read front-page stories of the Graf Zeppelin's trip around the world, Lindbergh's marriage to Anne Morrow, Richard Byrd's trip to the South Pole. George Temple admired the day's dominant sports figures, Babe Ruth, Bill Tilden and Bobby Jones. The Temple boys, Jack and George, excitedly followed the wars of Chicago gangsters, led by Al Capone, who drove armored cars and carried guns slung under their left arm pits.

Armies of Federal agents under Mabel Walker Willebrandt pursued violators of the Volstead Act, but bootleggers and hijackers flourished. In speak-easies, visitors who were able to identify themselves bought green liquor at $1 a shot, and Texas Guinan greeted visitors to her night club with a raucous "Hello, sucker!" Thousands went blind from wood alcohol. Etta Mae Miller, mother of ten, was jailed for life as a habitual offender after four convictions for selling liquor. Liquor shipments were disguised as ink, paint, olive oil and meat sauce. Boats were christened with grape juice.

Like most other Americans, the Temples took scant interest in foreign affairs. Manchuria was still a Chinese province, and Hirohito had sat for less than a year on the Japanese throne. Mussolini was much admired for his efficiency. Germany was governed by President von Hindenburg, and few Americans had heard of a small reactionary party led by Adolf Hitler. Sixty-two nations, including Germany and Italy, had signed the Kellogg-Briand Pact outlawing war.

This was the world into which Shirley Temple was born—a world whose precarious crust of security broke almost before she was old enough to talk. In October, 1929, came the sickening thunder of falling stocks. Fortunes melted between lunch time and dinner. Brokers jumped from New York skyscrapers, and in Chicago there were so many suicides from the great balcony in Marshall Field's that the store kept a life crew ready with a net. In two months, fifteen billion dollars' worth of stock values disappeared. Every morning, George Temple's bank opened its doors to a line of depositors waiting to withdraw money. A few years later the studio publicity department began calling Shirley "our depression baby."

Through the years of Shirley's babyhood, the depression deepened. By 1932, Americans were getting half the income in wages, dividends and salaries which they had received before the crash. Bankrupts sold apples on cold street corners. Fourteen million men were jobless. Shantytowns, called Hoovervilles, sprang up outside cities. Millions would have starved without free soup kitchens. Thousands did anyway. Overseas, Japan took Manchuria, and in Germany Adolf Hitler became Chancellor, abolished all political parties except the Nazis and launched his drive against the Jews.

Americans like the Temples, who were able to keep their heads above the black whirlpool of depression, played miniature golf and backgammon, listened to Amos 'n' Andy, talked about whether Jean Harlow's platinum hair was natural, followed the championship bridge match of the Culbertsons versus Sidney Lenz and Oswald Jacoby, and tried to understand Howard Scott's philosophy of technocracy. With the rest of the nation, the Temples turned eagerly to their morning papers during the ten weeks when the Lindbergh "eaglet," stolen from his crib in his white sleeping suit, was missing, and Gertrude Temple cried when the baby was found dead.

The wind-blown bob, with its short points of hair plastered against the cheeks, gave way to more gracious coiffures, under coy, beplumed Empress Eugénie hats. Suddenly the boyish figure disappeared. Waistlines returned to normal, skirts were full enough to walk in, curls and ruffles were no longer *déclassé*.

In 1932 George and Gertrude Temple, sitting up late to hear the election returns, learned that Franklin Roosevelt, running with Jack Garner, had been elected President. Monday, after the inauguration, George Temple came home early and announced that the bank was closed. In a 99-day session, Congress passed the Emergency Banking Act, the AAA, the TVA, the CCC, the Home Owners' Loan Act, and the Gold Clause resolution. The blue eagles of NRA appeared in shop windows, hoarders were urged to turn in gold, and the words "New Deal" were more frequently uttered than any other phrase in the language.

A Century of Progress, headlined by the fan dancer, Sally Rand, opened in Chicago. Newspapers frontpaged the picture of a midget sitting on J. P. Morgan's lap. *Anthony Adverse* was a best seller. Bank night and pin-ball machines entered the American scene. Three point two beer became legal, and earnest drinkers grimly tried to absorb an effective amount of the mild beverage. Total repeal followed. America was trying to forget its troubles.

Meanwhile, there had been revolution in the movies. Shortly before Shirley Temple's birth, Warner Brothers had purchased the Vitaphone, a device for recording actors' voices, and had produced the first talking picture, *The Jazz Singer,* starring Al Jolson. It grossed two million. Within a year, theaters were wired for sound, every actor in the business except Rin-Tin-Tin began taking voice lessons, and American stars with American voices replaced most foreign luminaries.

By the time Shirley Temple's career began, the silent picture was archaic. Greta Garbo and John Gilbert were starred in *Queen Christina.* Charles Laughton won the Academy Award for *The Private Life of Henry VIII.* Mickey Mouse was a national figure, audiences were ecstatic over *The Three Little Pigs,* and everyone was humming "Who's Afraid of the Big Bad Wolf?" The Fred Astaire-Ginger Rogers dancing team made its debut in *Flying Down to Rio.* Mae West uttered her immortal "C'm up and see me sometime," and *It Happened One Night* was in production. The talking picture was ready for Shirley.

Without realizing it, the American public was also ready for Shirley Temple. Frightened by the depression, divided among themselves about the best means to combat it, listening to the threat of war drums beating louder and louder across both oceans, Americans were worried. They needed escape, the type of escape which was to be provided by the joyous fantasy of Shirley's pictures. During the next eight years, the plots of her films were to be better known, from continent to continent, than the story of Edward VIII's romance with Wallis Warfield, and her baby dimples were to be more familiar than Adolf Hitler's mustache or the umbrella which Neville Chamberlain carried to Munich.

Baby's Name _Shirley Jane Temple_

_____ was born at _9:00 P.M._ o'clock

on _April 23rd_ _____ 1928

Place _Santa Monica Hospital,_

Mother's Signature _Gertrude Temple_

Father's Signature _____ _Temple_

Doctor's Signature _Leo J. Madsen M.D._

Nurse's Signature _____

	Weight	Height
At birth	6½ lbs.	1 ft. 8 in.
One month	8 "	21 in. "
Two months	10 "	21¾ in. "
Three "	11½ "	22½ in. "
Four "	13½ "	23 in. "
Five "	14½ "	24 in. "
Six "	15½ "	25 in. "
One year	19½ "	28½ in. "
Two years	26 "	32 in. "
Three "	37½ "	36 in. "
Four "	37½ "	40 in. "
Five "	43 "	43 in. "

❧ Important Events ❧

First Sun Bath – 4 mo. old.

First time Baby stood with help	First time Baby walked with help

Stood up and walked around play pen at 9 mo.

First time Baby stood without help	First time Baby walked without help

May 31 - '29 – 13 mo. 1 wk

First Tooth   **First Word**

ma-ma - 7½ mo.   Baw-Wow ⎫ 9 mo.

June 3 - '29   13 mo.-11 days.   Da-Da - 8½ mo.   Bye-Bye ⎭

Words at 1 year.   **First Sentence** at 1 year – Don't do a'h –

Tickle - Tickle   ma-ma   da-da   What's that

Hello   Bye-Bye   Baw-Wow   All gone   Stop.

Bang-Bang   Oh Yes   Pretty   Baby   Yum-Yum

Shirley at 8 months. She was playing in the yard of her Santa Monica home when her father took this snapshot for the family album. This was in December of 1928 when the "Hoover bull market" broke sharply only to right itself for a further dizzy climb.

24

Shirley at 1½ years. These pictures were taken in a professional photographer's studio. A few years later, pictures like these were used as models for Shirley Temple baby dolls, a popular addition to the Shirley doll line.

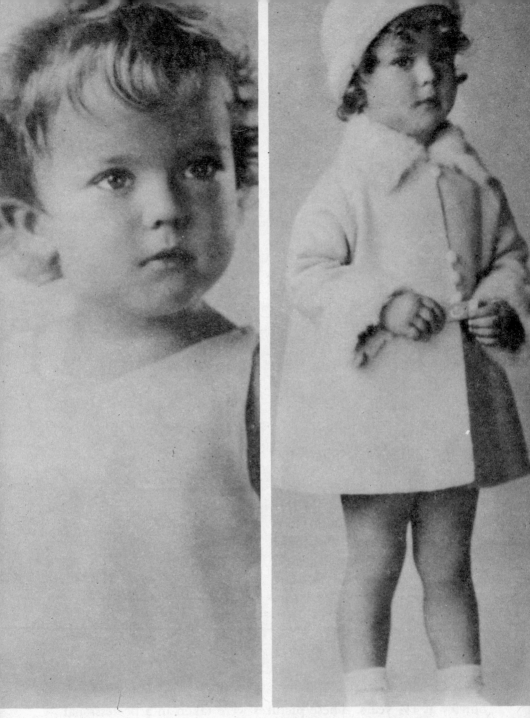

The pictures on this spread show Shirley at 2, 2½, 3, and 3½ years of age. Final picture in the series shows Shirley as she looked when a film talent scout noticed her in a children's dancing class and

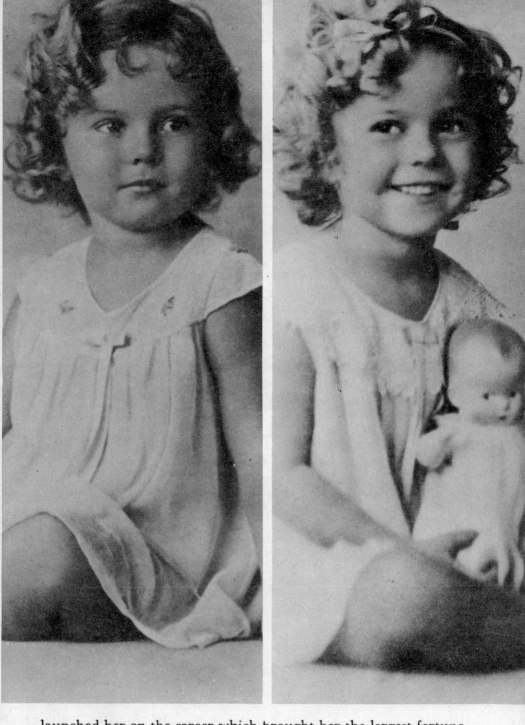

launched her on the career which brought her the largest fortune
ever earned by a child—earned, incidentally, during the grimmest
years of the depression.

Shirley in the back yard of the house where she was born.

CHAPTER 1

How It Began

Beginning this book, I feel almost the way I did at school the first time my class put on an amateur play. Every girl in the place had stage fright, but I, with only a bit part, turned the greenest. I'd been in front of a camera hundreds of times, but waiting for that curtain to go up, with an assortment of everybody's friends and relatives out in front, was a horse of a different hue. Same way now. I've given plenty of interviews, but speaking for myself makes me a little quivery, just to start out with. Still, I've had such a divine life so far that it's worth recording, so here goes.

Mom swears I was a beautiful baby, but as far as anyone else's opinion goes, I was strictly standard brand. But I did please the whole family right away by turning out to be female. Mom, who already had two boys, wanted a girl so badly that before I was born, Daddy and the doctor considered leaving town in case I turned out to be a boy. They were afraid she would hold them responsible.

Jack was 12 and George was 8 when I arrived upon the scene, and the family lived in a cute little house in Santa Monica. Daddy was a bank manager and made what is known as a modest salary, which means that there was enough money to feed everybody and keep the rent paid, but not enough for "lily-gilding." Mom did her own housework and she made practically all my baby clothes.

My two brothers always made a great fuss over me, because I

was so much younger, and I've always been crazy about both of them. We've never come to blows about anything, except for a few Sunday morning squabbles over the funnies which I used to hide away to "read" later. I must say they had the law on their side because I was still learning my ABC's at that time. Mom says that Jack, my older brother, used to take nearly as much care of me as she did. When Mom and Daddy went out evenings, they'd hire a baby sitter to stay with me, and Jack always got in a tizzy for fear she'd neglect me, so finally the family solved the problem by leaving Jack in charge. If I cried, he'd put on Mom's bathrobe and go in to pick me up, to deceive my youthful innocence into thinking he was Mom in person.

Of course, there isn't much I can remember about those days. Mom and I were together all day because the boys were at school and I was all she had to worry about. I do remember prancing around the room to music from the radio which was on a good deal of the time. Mom used to sing and dance with me because she loved it as much as I did. I guess I was dancing before I actually learned to walk. Almost every noon Mom would teach me my ABC's while we ate lunch together. Thanks to her "lessons," I knew parts of the multiplication table, and the number of days in the week and months in the year before I was 3.

When I reached the age of 3, Mom decided that it would be fun for me to go to dancing school. She'd wanted to dance when she was a girl, but her family was so conservative that she wasn't allowed to, so she planned to give me the fun she had missed. One of Daddy's customers in the bank had a very nice dancing school with a class for tiny tots and every week Mom took me there for my lesson. She watched from the side lines with the other mothers while we all tripped merrily around the floor. Oh, how I loved those dancing lessons!

I remember dancing class very clearly, especially the day the movie scout came in, because that was how I started making movies. There was a lot of excitement that day and the whole class was dressed up in their best clothes when I arrived in an old dancing dress. When Mom discovered they expected a movie scout who was looking for child talent, we left. She had the car started, ready to go home, when my teacher came out and asked her if she would let the movie scout see me. I wanted her to come in with me but she had to stay outside with the other mothers while 30 or 40 of us paraded up and down for the movie scout. The next week while we were all leaping around, pretending to be butterflies or something, another man came in to look us over. I remembered the last time the movie scout came and made us just stand around, so another little girl and I hid behind the piano. The man saw our feet and coaxed us to come out. It was Charles Lamont of Educational Pictures, looking for 25 children to play in a *Baby Burlesks* series they were going to make, and he picked me!

Mom was amused and puzzled when they told her they would like to use me in their series. Neither she nor Daddy would have thought of such a thing, since the family had never had any connections with the theater and amusement world, but she was pleased, too, being a typically proud parent. She had a hard time persuading Daddy, who was strenuously opposed to the whole thing, but he was curious about how I would look on the screen so we finally won him over.

Mom took me to the Educational Studio and then the fun started. You never saw so many mothers and children in your life as there were on the set for the *Baby Burlesks*. Children yelling, and children having their noses blown, and children getting into fights with one another. Mom and I sort of stayed on the side lines, but apparently I was the right shape and size for one of the leading parts, so I was cast right off for my first "important" role. Of all things, it was a burlesque of Dolores Del Rio in *What Price Glory*.

The *Baby Burlesks* were one-reel take-offs on famous motion pictures, with tiny children playing all the parts. The phenomenal success of Hal Roach's *Our Gang Comedies* had made child movies sure-fire at the box office. *Baby Burlesks* were shot in four days. At $10 a day I wasn't doing badly for a 3-year-old in the middle of a depression! We made them in such rapid succession that I soon had a nice little nest egg, carefully put aside by Mom and Daddy. I carried the "leading-lady" roles which were heavily costumed but a little sketchy on dialogue. The first words I spoke on the screen, strange as it seems, were French. I said, "Mais oui, mon cher." Naturally, I didn't know what the funny sounds meant, and my accent must have been something.

All of us wore very elaborate costumes, authentic grown-up clothes from the waist up and diapers pinned with enormous safety pins. Mom worked much harder than I did because she had to make all my costumes and press them at night. She created a special panty for me with a flap in front that resembled a diaper. This was to pacify George and Jack, who objected to the diapers. She spent her days on the set with me and considering the four-day shooting schedule, they must have been nightmares.

One of my roles was a take-off of Marlene Dietrich billed as "Morelegs Sweetrick," wearing lots of blue feathers and sequins which I considered really dreamy. That's probably the most sirenish outfit I've ever worn on the screen, though I hope I'll get another glamour role before I'm through. Then, for another picture, they put me in a big, gold bird cage, and I sang "I'm Only a Bird in a Gilded Cage." In *War Babies* we drank milk out of French wine jugs and wore doughboy uniforms and overseas caps. All this for $10 a day and did I love it!

I was mad about the other children, and mad about the costumes, and I was absolutely ecstatic about the studio. A movie lot is a fascinating place even for grownups, but for a child it's completely Alice-in-Wonderland. Machines and gadgets all over, trees and grass apparently growing right inside a building, men walking on little bridges up in the air—and never a dull moment! Mom had never been on a studio lot before, so she was as agog about it as I was. It took us quite a while to stop asking foolish questions.

Shirley was born and grew up in this Santa Monica bungalow.

Jack Hays, above, was Shirley's first employer at Educational.
When she became a star at Fox, Hays sued for a share of her earnings, claiming she was under contract to him, but lost the suit.

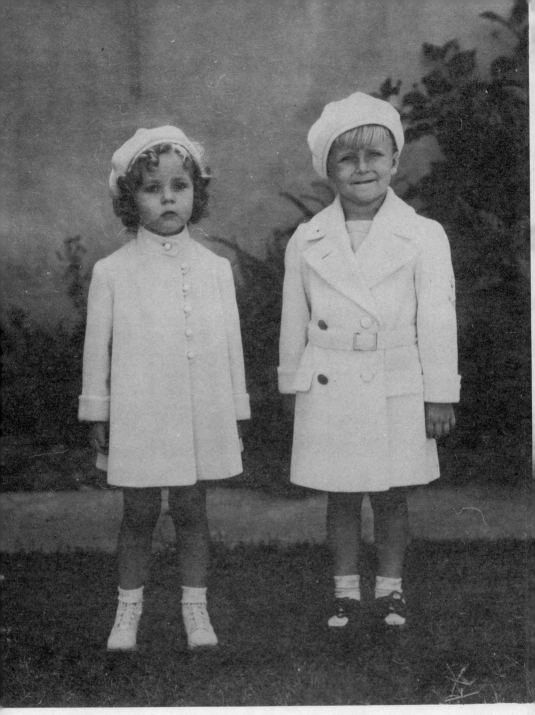

With Shirley is Georgie Smith, who played opposite her in several of Educational's *Baby Burlesks*. Of the child stars popular during Shirley's babyhood, only Dickie Moore stayed in the movies.

Lampooning Hollywood adventure films, Shirley brings civiliza-
tion to darkest Africa. To capitalize on comic contrast, "natives"
wear grass skirts, war paint and sneakers.

One of Shirley's first roles was a burlesque of Marlene Dietrich.

Outstanding among Educational's child players, she was featured in their advertising, given a prominent position in publicity stills.

Posing for publicity stills without seeming to pose is an art Shirley had not mastered at 3½. Despite her inexperience, she showed early the charm that would one day place her pictures in countless news-papers and magazines all over America.

The Pie-Covered Wagon, one of the first *Baby Burlesks,* was a take-off on *The Covered Wagon.* Full-sized sets and props dwarf Shirley

and her leading man, add to the comedy. The diaper and safety pin worn by both children were gags used throughout the entire series.

This is Shirley with Baby Le Roy. At 17, she has never been cast as a vamp, but when she looks back to costumes like this she writes, "I hope I'll get another glamour role before I'm through."

Production still from one of the *Baby Burlesks,* which were sub-titled "Kiddin' Hollywood." Shirley is playing a slavey who is "dis-covered" by films. The three "yes men" in the background satirized an old Hollywood tradition.

Before Shirley was 5, Mrs. Temple had designed her famous, widely imitated coiffure. Shirley's hair is naturally curly so it was an easy task for her mother to comb it, making each ringlet on a finger.

41

Shirley and Georgie Smith pose beside a poster showing Shirley in the Marlene Dietrich costume which she calls "the most sirenish outfit I've ever worn on the screen." Playing opposite "Morelegs Sweetrick" was "Frightwig Von Stumblebum." The marks in the cement are actually on the famous court of Grauman's Chinese Theater in Hollywood, where stars sign their names in soft cement.

Shirley Temple looked like this at 4 years. No one could foresee that in a few years Shirley actually would be asked to print her name on the cement at Grauman's.

Between scenes, Mrs. Temple reads to Shirley. Directors, whenever possible, exploited Shirley's childish appeal by including a scene which showed her in pajamas like these.

CHAPTER 2

Up to Stardom

Coincidence is a big thing in anybody's life, it seems to "Old Granny Temple." There were three coincidences at the start of my movie career, and without them I'm not sure there would have been any career at all. The first was when that talent scout happened to visit my dancing class. The second put me under contract to Fox, and the third led to my being in *Little Miss Marker,* which made me a star.

After several months, during which I made six one-reel pictures for Educational, I was graduated to a series of short films called *Frolics of Youth.* I played the little sister in these teen-age two-reelers after Educational finished *Baby Burlesks.* We had made four films in the series when my career was abruptly changed one rainy Saturday. We had gone to the neighborhood picture show and had just seen a preview of the fourth picture of this series. Mom and I stood under the marquee while Daddy brought the car around for us. As we were waiting, a man came up and introduced himself. He was Jay Gorney, and he'd written the music for *Stand Up and Cheer,* which Fox was going to produce. It was just plain Fox in those days, without the Twentieth Century.

They were testing scads of little girls for a part in the picture, and Mr. Gorney had seen me on the screen and thought I should have a chance at it. He asked Mom if I could sing, and she said she guessed so, and he said someone from Fox would call us up.

They didn't call for several weeks, and Mom had practically forgotten about it when they did. She took me over to the studio where we met Mr. Lew Brown who was the associate producer of the picture. He took me to a beautiful big office where I met Mr. Winfield Sheehan, Fox vice-president, who really started me on my career. He signed me up and became both my friend and mentor.

Stand Up and Cheer was quite a movie. It had a plot like nothing on earth. At this time, the depression was rolling along superbly, and the picture was based on the idea of having the President appoint a Secretary of Amusement to cheer people up. Said Secretary promptly goes to work booking entertainers to ship around the country and cheer everybody up, which gave Fox a chance to promote many musical numbers. Then the plot thickens like tapioca, because it seems there's a dangerous group of crooks whose fortunes mysteriously depend on the depression's continuing, and they try to ruin everything. Naturally, it turns out all right. I loved the picture even if it was on the zany side, because it was the start of my great romance with Jimmy Dunn.

We had a swell song-and-dance number. I came in at the close of it, making my appearance by crawling out from between Jimmy's legs, and joined him in the finale. The studio decided that it would be easier for me to teach Jimmy the dance routine I knew already than for me to learn something different, so my very first job at Fox was giving Jimmy Dunn dancing lessons. What impressed me most at the first rehearsal, next to that famous Dunn charm, was the towel that Jimmy wore around his neck so he wouldn't catch cold if he became overheated. Most dancers do that at rehearsals, but I'd never seen it before, and I couldn't get over it.

After Jimmy and I had rehearsed our dance for about a week, Mr. Brown gave Mom an envelope with the words of the chorus of the song I was to sing scribbled on it. I had learned the tune while doing the dance. The next day was set for recording. In the movies, it's customary to make the recording of a song first, with its musical background, and then someone plays the recording back while you go through the motions of singing before the camera.

We went to our dressing room around one o'clock on that eventful day, and we waited and waited. I grew very sleepy because it was past my nap time, so Mom decided I should have a little rest. I hadn't been asleep more than fifteen minutes when they called for me, so up I got, all sleepy-eyed, and we went over to the recording room. This recording room was enormous, and the orchestra was enormous, and there were 50 chorus girls in slinky black costumes sitting around the walls. This was the first time I had ever seen an orchestra.

I was pretty tiny so they stood me on a table in front of the microphone I was to sing into. We rehearsed once and then made two recordings and in half an hour it was over. Harold Lloyd told Mom after he watched this recording that a feminine Jackie Coogan had been found. Mom and I thought it was all quite ordinary, but apparently everyone, including the director, was impressed because I had made two okay recordings after a single rehearsal. Mr. Brown came over and picked me up and said to Mom, "Is this child under contract?" Mom said I'd been signed up for just that one picture. They immediately wanted a long term contract, so they hustled to get Mom's and Daddy's signature on the dotted line, and from then on Fox and I were partners.

If I live to be 145, I'll never forget the preview of *Stand Up and Cheer*. It was a matinee and Daddy couldn't go but Mom took me and her best friend, Mrs. Ferguson. We went over to pick her up and then, just as we were ready to start, somehow or other I locked myself in the bathroom. Mom knocked and called for me to come out or we'd be late, and I tried and tried to get the door open, but I just couldn't.

Fortunately, the bathroom window was open. Mrs. Ferguson put a ladder against the wall of the house and pulled me out through the window (all dressed up in my best bib and tucker) and off we went. At that point, I think Mom had grave doubts about whether my being in the movies was worth such a to-do. Apparently this locking oneself in the bathroom is a Temple trait because my little nephew, Stanley, was recently rescued from a similar predicament.

Another time my movie career backfired a little was when a Fox photographer came out to take pictures of me playing at home. When he plugged in the big floodlights to light up our living room, it was too much for the wiring system in the house and a fuse blew out. Mom didn't know how to fix it, so we were blacked-out until Daddy got home.

Also, we'd just gotten a new icebox which was everyone's pride and joy, including my brothers, Jack and George, but unfortunately it couldn't operate without electricity. The day was hot, and by the time Daddy fixed the fuse, everything in the icebox was spoiled, including a prize chicken which Mom was going to roast for Sunday.

After *Stand Up and Cheer*, Fox wasn't quite sure how to handle me, because it wasn't easy to find good parts for anyone my age and size. Mr. Sheehan took a personal interest in me and protected me with special orders in the studio. He wouldn't let me eat in the Fox commissary for fear the other actors would spoil me. His idea was that I should take small parts until I got a little older and built up a following. So I played bits in *Change of Heart* and *Now I'll Tell.* Then came *Little Miss Marker,* which was the third big coincidence in my movie career.

Mom and I were at Western Costumes having a fitting for *Stand Up and Cheer* and were near the Paramount studio when Mom remembered a man who had been especially nice to us when I'd taken a tiny part in a Western picture there. She asked me if I'd like to drop in and say hello, and being the sociable type, I was all for it. So in we went, and while we were there somebody suggested that we see the casting director. Mom explained that I was under contract to Fox, and she was greatly surprised to learn that a studio would often loan out a player to another studio. So I went in to see the director, Al Hall, on the theory that we had nothing to lose but five minutes.

Mom waited outside, and naturally enough she couldn't help listening. She heard Mr. Hall's voice without being able to tell what he said, and then through the half open door she heard me say very clearly, "Aw, nuts." She waited and worried, and after a minute she heard me say "Scram!" This really worried her, but everything was explained when Mr. Hall and I came out. He'd been testing me for the part of "Marky" in *Little Miss Marker,* the Damon Runyon story. It was a three-word test, and I guess I passed, because Paramount asked Fox if it could borrow me for the part.

Then there were delays and delays and delays. Fox wasn't sure whether it wanted to loan me or not. All my clothes were designed and fitted at Paramount, and I learned my whole part, and still Fox didn't sign. Finally it agreed that I could go to Paramount as soon as I finished my part in *Change of Heart*, and then there were more delays and delays because they didn't get around to shooting the scenes in which I appeared.

Meanwhile, Paramount was holding up the production of *Little Miss Marker*. Then at long last Fox called us up on a Saturday afternoon and told Mom that if Monday was rainy, so that the cameramen couldn't do any outdoor shooting on *Change of Heart*, they could make the scene in which I appeared, which was indoors. Mom prayed for rain all day Sunday, and sure enough, Monday it was pouring.

We went over to Fox and I played the scene, which turned out to be very brief. I didn't even have to take off the hat and coat I was wearing. There was a big airplane on the set and I looked at it admiringly, and somebody handed me a small paper airplane, and I took it and grinned, and that was that. By noon I was home eating my soup and vegetables, and next day we reported to Paramount and I started *Little Miss Marker*, which is supposed to be one of the best pictures I ever made as a child.

Little Miss Marker was a real tear-jerker. I played the part of a little girl who was left by her father as the marker, or security, on a race-track ticket. When the horse, "Dream Prince," lost the race, my father disappeared and I was informally adopted by Adolphe Menjou, called "Sorrowful" in the picture. I named "Sorrowful" and his gang after the members of King Arthur's Court whom I adored. Without a copy of the *Legends* at hand, "Sorrowful" read a variation on the King Arthur story to me out of track magazines until I began to pick up race-track slang. "Bangles," who was "Sorrowful's" sweetheart, worried about the change in me and persuaded him to stage a medieval pageant which would restore my faith in fairy tales. All of the gang dressed up as Knights of the Round Table and I was riding "Dream Prince" around the night club they had hired for the occasion when "Big Steve" walked in. "Big Steve" was the heavy in the picture, played by Charles Bickford.

"Dream Prince" reared when he saw him and I was thrown. They rushed me to the hospital and saved me with a transfusion from "Big Steve," who was converted on the operating table. "Bangles" and "Sorrowful" were reunited and everybody lived happily ever after.

Far as I was concerned, the high point in making *Little Miss Marker* was the scene in which I had to be thrown off a horse. I'd never ridden a horse before, but my adoration for them dates from that moment. I wore a form-fitting canvas jacket lined with lamb's-wool and they rigged up a contraption of piano wire, which is invisible on the screen, and put it on me so I wouldn't get hurt when I fell. It was super. I'd fly off the horse into the air and land like a feather. The director had to remind me not to grin because I enjoyed the flight so much. They made only one rehearsal and one take on that scene, but I would have been perfectly content to do retakes all day long. Mom says I loved the costumes for that picture so much I cried when I had to take off the last one.

Adolphe Menjou was wonderful to work with and he used to play jacks with me on the dressing-room floor. The studio would never allow any photographs made of our games because it might destroy his reputation as "Hollywood's best-dressed man." He played hide-and-seek with me, too, but that game ended the day he sailed over a portable fence to land on his face. Everybody had lots of fun making *Little Miss Marker*.

Immortalized in this life-sized wax figure, Shirley was the model for thousands of Temple dolls sold in stores all over the nation.

This scene from *Stand Up and Cheer* brought Shirley Temple to
Hollywood's attention as a potential star. It was her first appearance with Jimmy Dunn (foreground) and the beginning of what
she calls "my great romance" with him. Shirley entered the scene

for the finale song-and-dance number called "Daddy Take a Bow."
Audiences remembered Shirley's bit part longer than the film's
lavish production and big names. Cashing in on this early hit, the
studio brought out a later picture called "Baby Take a Bow."

Hollywood publicity men did not miss the opportunity to photograph Shirley opening an account with her Fox salary check at the Los Angeles bank of which her father, above, was manager. Right, Shirley drinks milk from a tin cup while working on loca-

tion at Lake Arrowhead, near Hollywood. She greatly enjoyed
working on location, and when she was told that the company
would be at Lake Arrowhead for twenty-one days, exclaimed,
"Goody, twenty-one box lunches!"

On Shirley's behalf, her parents sign her first long-term contract with Fox.

Shirley celebrates her fifth birthday with a children's party in the Fox studio café, first of many such celebrations.

This room in Shirley's bungalow on the Fox lot served as her kindergarten. The color scheme was bright blue and white.

This is an exterior view of Shirley's bungalow, where she lunched, napped, played and studied during her career at Fox.

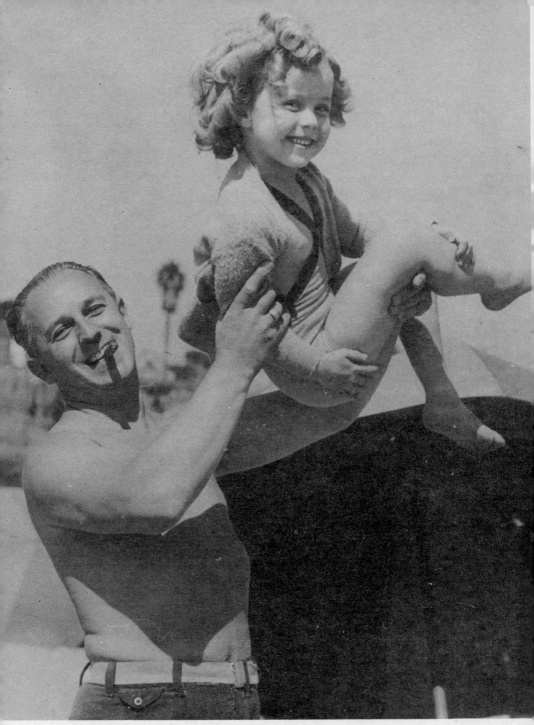

Shirley's close, affectionate relationship with her parents and brothers was a fact, not an invention of fan magazine writers. Above, Shirley and her father enjoy a holiday on the beach at Santa Monica.

The Temple family is still knit together by exceptionally close ties. Above, Shirley spends a quiet evening at home looking at pictures with her older brothers, Jack, left, and George.

Left, Shirley poses with the judge who approved her first long-term contract with Fox. Right, with Will Rogers, also a Fox star, who had a bungalow on the lot close to hers. Plans made by Fox to star Shirley and Rogers together were cancelled by his death in 1935. Shirley's first radio appearance and her first public appearance were both made for the benefit of the Will Rogers Memorial Fund.

Dickie Moore and Shirley have a tea party with puppet figures of Minnie and Mickey Mouse, used in a Hollywood puppet show.

Shirley does an impromptu hula on the beach, playing an imaginary ukulele. A natural imitator, she picked up the hula by watching a dancer at Fox. Later, in *Captain January*, the studio wanted to have her dance a hula, but concluded from fan letters that her audiences would consider it too sophisticated for a little girl.

LITTLE
MISS MARKER

This was Shirley's first starring role. She played the part of a youngster whose father had left her with some race track touts as security (a "marker") on a racing ticket. When her father fails to claim her, "Sorrowful," the leader of the gang, played by Adolphe Menjou, adopts her, calls her "Marky."

1. "Sorrowful" turns "Marky" over to a tout who steals a barber pole she thinks is candy.

4. He grudgingly pays for clothes "Bangles," the girl of the gang, ordered for "Marky" . . .

5. . . . buys an orthodox King Arthur which fails to enchant "Marky" after the *Racing Form*.

2. Not knowing what to do with his protégée when she turns up his buried king at poker . . .

3. . . . "Sorrowful" reads her the *Racing Form,* names the jockeys after King Arthur's knights.

6. "Big Steve," the heavy, leaves "Bangles" in "Sorrowful's" care, goes to Chicago.

7. The change in "Marky" worries "Bangles" who has by now fallen in love with "Sorrowful."

8. The gang stages a pageant which fails to restore "Marky's" faith in fairy tales . . .

9. . . . until "Dream Prince," a real race horse, is brought to life right out of *King Arthur*.

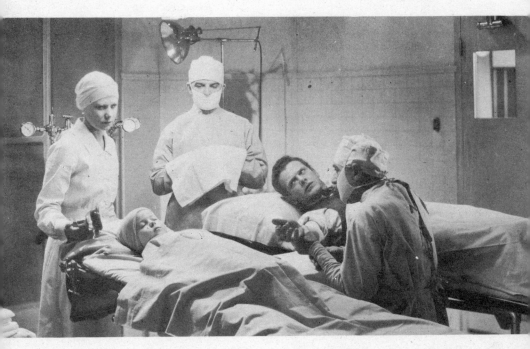

12. Touched by "Marky's" recovery, "Big Steve" decides to turn over a new leaf, gives up "Bangles" to "Sorrowful" who, he knows, has always loved her. "Marky" is saved by the transfusion . . .

10. But the "charger" shies, throwing "Marky." A blood transfusion is needed to save her.

11. Nobody has the right type blood except "Big Steve" who gives his at the point of a gun.

13. ... the reluctant lovers are brought together, and "Marky" has found a mother and father ... setting the traditional happy ending for many a Temple picture to come.

Marilyn Granas, described by Shirley as "a very cute little girl with bangs," was her stand-in for *Now and Forever,* in which, critics considered, Shirley stole scenes from Gary Cooper and Carole Lombard.

CHAPTER 3

Acting Is Fun

Nobody was surprised that *Little Miss Marker* clicked, because it was a swell picture, but what took Mom off her feet was the copy of *Variety* somebody sent her from New York. It had a headline saying "Temple Holds 'Em Three Weeks." It took Mom several minutes to realize that this Temple character was her little Shirley. When she did realize it, she knew that I was in the movies to stay, and that it was probably going to be a big thing. It scared her, and I suspect it scared Daddy a bit, too, though he'd never admit it. Of course, I wasn't scared. I dare anyone to say "No sense, no feeling."

Everything began to pop at once. A man at Educational started to sue us, claiming that he'd discovered and trained me and ought to have a healthy slice of my earnings. Fortunately, the court didn't see it that way. Fox signed me up on another, longer contract, and a couple of manufacturers asked if they could put out a line of Shirley Temple dolls and dresses. We began getting piles of fan mail, and people stopped us on the street and asked "Isn't that little Shirley Temple?" The children's accounts at Daddy's bank went up something like 500 per cent. It was pretty bewildering for a family that had never had anything to do with movies until just a year or so before.

At that point, I'm sure there were a lot of family conferences going on over my head. The family had to work out a policy on money, because by this time Fox was paying me quite a lot—Mom never told me how much and I never wanted to know. Mom and Daddy decided to put everything I earned into a trust fund, and that any improvements in the family style of living should come from the salary the studio paid Mom to teach me my lines and look after me generally, plus Daddy's salary. They stuck to this policy straight through, which isn't always done in the movies, because lots of parents feel that whatever their children earn belongs to them.

At first there were very few changes in the way we lived. We moved to another house in Santa Monica, which Mom and Daddy had previously been planning to do. Mom got a housekeeper, since she had to be at the studio with me nearly every day. George went to military school, which had been the dream of his young life, and very swank he looked in his uniform. But no butler, no champagne parties, no Rolls-Royce—as a matter of fact, to this day we're still driving around in a station wagon—my pride and joy.

Mom and Daddy had never known any picture people, and even when movies got to be the biggest thing in our lives, they didn't go with that group. They're still going with the same friends they had when Daddy was in the banking business, mostly business-men and their wives. I don't go with many movie people either, with a few exceptions, of course, like Zasu Pitts' son and daughter who live next door, and Harold Lloyd's daughters, who were upperclass girls at my school. It isn't a policy; it just happened that way. But it's just as well, because movie people talk movies, and it's nice to get away from your job evenings and weekends.

Mom took great pains to keep me from getting false ideas about being a great big, glamorous movie genius. When we went to my first première, I asked her if it was an honor for me to be going to a première of my picture. She replied that it was a great honor for the picture and that I was a very lucky girl to be in it. If people stopped us on the street, she'd say they liked me because I was polite and friendly, had a clean face and hands, and looked happy. Once when we were on Balboa Island some boys caught a great big fish, and when people gathered around, Mom said they were look-ing at the fish, which thrilled me far more than if I'd thought they were looking at me, because the fish was truly stupendous.

The Fox people, especially Mr. Winfield Sheehan, were also very anxious that I shouldn't become spoiled, because if I started admiring myself, it would be sure to come out on the screen. "It would show in the eyes," said Mr. Sheehan. No one was allowed to ask me to dance or recite, and no one was supposed to congratulate me on my work except the director. Mom and I were not allowed to eat in the Fox café, where all the studio people ate, for fear I'd grow up too fast. Mom has always said that the fine advice given her by Mr. Winfield Sheehan in the early stages of my career was the greatest help she had.

There was a studio-wide conspiracy to keep me from getting sophisticated. Once when John Ford was directing a picture I was in, a man on the set started to swear, and Mr. Ford actually made him stand in a corner for five minutes. He must have felt like an awful fool, but as things turned out, he had his revenge. A couple of days later, John Ford uttered a mildly profane word, and I made him stand in the corner, much to the ecstatic joy of the workman who had previously been punished. However, they were both in pretty fine company because even Mom herself had to take a turn in the corner one day.

My contract had special provisions which were meant to protect me. There had to be a guard with me to keep me from getting hurt, and Mom and Daddy were bound to respect his wishes whenever he thought my safety was involved. Also, there were provisions that nobody but Mom should fix my hair, and that I should never be asked to wear make-up, and that I was never to take any dramatic lessons.

All these precautions really made me take being in the movies very much for granted. When Mom and I started off to the studio every morning, she explained to me that I was going to school just like Jack and George, only in a different direction, and that was the way I looked at it. Now, when I look back, it seems to me that I was one of the luckiest and happiest little girls in the world. Not because I was a star, for at that time I didn't know the meaning of the word, but because I had so many wonderful friends and so much fun.

Movies really are terrific fun. To me they were always a great big gorgeous game of let's-pretend. Children spend most of their time pretending to be somebody else anyhow, and the people who used to talk about my "acting ability" just didn't realize that make-believe is the most natural thing in the world for a child. But for me it was special fun because I had a studio full of people to play with me and all the costumes and scenery I needed.

Often I did just the same things for the camera that any little girl does at home. For instance, in *Bright Eyes,* I played at being a grown-up lady, with a long dress and a doll to push in a baby carriage. And then I was a very old lady, with spectacles and tiny wrinkles put on my face and hands by the make-up man. I had hair-raising adventures with the Yankee army in *The Littlest Rebel.* In *Wee Willie Winkie* I played soldier, with a drum and kilt made of real Black Watch plaid and a squadron of soldiers to march with. In this picture I learned the English manual of arms and instead of reading *Heidi,* like most girls, I acted it out. It wasn't work, it was play.

As for Grif, my guard, I regarded him as simply a tall man who carried a marvelous pair of handcuffs in his pocket. There was so much that could be done with those handcuffs. You could beg them away from Grif and handcuff people to chairs or handcuff yourself. Once I persuaded Mr. Seiter, one of the Fox directors, to lie down and be handcuffed. He entered into the spirit of the thing very well, and writhed and groaned quite realistically, but when he got bored and wanted to be released, he found that a prop man who was my fellow conspirator had hidden the key. I'd have kept Mr. Seiter in the handcuffs all day if it had been left to me, but unfortunately his authority over the prop man was such that the key had to be given back.

Looking through the camera, and listening to sound through the earphones, was lots of fun. When the assistant cameraman measured the distance from the camera to the actors with his tape, he'd let me guess the footage. Sometimes when I guessed right he pretended I was wrong, and told me a fib about how long the tape really was, and then I'd get even by snarling it up. This was a ceremony we went through practically every day.

All in all, I regarded the Fox lot as a combination playground and school, and everybody on it was a playmate. It was especially fun when we made a picture with lots of other children, as in *Curly*

Top and *Heidi*. When we were making *Heidi*, everybody played pick-up-sticks. That's a game where you have a bunch of light wooden sticks, and you pile them up, and you have to pick them up one by one with a wire hook without moving any of the others. There were 40 or 50 of us all over the set playing jackstraws, and you couldn't put your foot down without stepping on a jackstraw belonging to some child.

I don't think I ever had a single misunderstanding with any of the other children in my pictures. Some writer started a story about a deadly feud between Jane Withers and me. Jane played with me in *Bright Eyes*. When Mom objected to this kind of publicity the writer said, "Well, if two little girls walk down the street hand in hand peacefully, no one notices, but if they're having a big fight, everybody stops and looks." Mom said she'd rather her little girl got along without publicity of that kind, but by this time the story had already been printed. Jane and I, as a matter of fact, got along fine.

People wouldn't really believe that I had time to play, and after I became well known, Mom used to receive worried letters asking if I ever had fun and if I wasn't getting old before my time. Once a fan magazine printed an absolutely heartbreaking story about me. It seems that one day I escaped from the house and went down to the beach and asked some children if they wouldn't please play with me. I took my bucket and spade and tried to build sand castles with the children, but they were so dazzled by my being in the movies that they refused. Then Mom came and took me back to my gilded jail. Actually, this or anything else like it, never happened.

The fact is, children don't seem to care about who is famous and who isn't. It's the parents who attach importance to such things. When I was a little girl, mothers would bring their children up to me and say, "Now, dear, tell little Shirley Temple how much you enjoyed her last picture." So the poor youngster would say, "I-enjoyed-your-last-picture-very-much." You could tell he'd learned it by heart.

Once in a restaurant a woman came up with a tiny little girl and said, "This girl has come all the way from New York to see you." She hid behind her mother's skirts in embarrassment, and I'm sure she never even saw me. We certainly couldn't see her, and her family must have been sorry they brought her all the way from New York for that.

Several times a year we would go down to Palm Springs, and have a complete rest from all studio photographers and publicity men. That is, except once. The studio had been getting so many letters asking if I was able to lead a normal life that they decided to make a group of photographs of me doing the things all children like to do. Until then my life in Palm Springs had been as normal as an ice-cream cone. But after the studio sent down their publicity man, I had to stop playing hide-and-seek and riding my pony and going swimming so that I could pose for pictures of myself playing hide-and-seek and riding my pony and going swimming. After they took all the pictures they wanted of me leading a normal life, I was able to go back to it. Not that I minded. The picture-taking lasted only one day, and the publicity man was Doc Bishop, one of my favorite chums, who made everything up to me by teaching me to ride a bicycle. Secretly, I believe that Doc wishes that he had never taught me to ride it, because, fearing that I might fall off, he ran along beside me for positively hours. The result—huge blisters.

Magazine stories really can be peculiar at times. Of all the stories ever circulated about me, the midget story was the funniest. How it got started, I couldn't say, but it reached a climax when an English magazine published an article revealing a secret that was definitely colossal. It seems I was a midget lady, thirty years old, with a midget husband. Of course, the only way to prove to everyone's satisfaction that you are not a midget is by growing up, which in due course I did.

Another story that isn't true is the electric-fence yard. We were supposed to have an electric fence around the house, for protection, after we moved from Santa Monica to Brentwood. Anyone who touched it would die like a dog, but at once. Well, if there'd been an electric fence around the yard where I played, I'd have died a thousand deaths. There actually is an automatic arrangement which opens the gate for people to drive in. You push a buzzer outside, and tell your name to Mom or Katie or me, and then we push a buzzer in the house to open the gate. Many people have gates of the same type.

Then there were quite a few magazine articles on how Mom brought me up, and most of them mentioned that when I was bad she spanked me. This was a concession to the spare-the-rod school because I don't remember Mom ever having spanked me at all. A hurt look could do a lot more with me than a spanking. In contrast, one big magazine ran an article saying I was a "peewee paragon" who always obeyed my mother, ate up all my spinach and carrots, and relished the taste of castor oil. Probably I did obey about as well as most girls, but the truth is that I never was given castor oil, and I hid my vegetables under my baked potato skin every time I thought I could get away with it.

Most of the people who wrote stories about me made me too good to be true, but at least once, a writer did a reverse and wrote a really mean article. It was when I was about 6. He said he'd come to the studio, and Mom had introduced him as a nice man who was going to write nice things about me, and after that I'd kissed him every time I saw him. A 6-year-old would have had to be a monster, it seems to me, to figure out a thing like that, and anyhow I never kissed people unless I knew them and was fond of them, and I'm even more choosy now. As for Mom, she wouldn't have dreamed of telling me that somebody was going to write about me.

Just a few months ago, when Mom and I were eating at the Brown Derby, the same character came up and apologized to us. Since I'd never seen the story, I didn't know what he was apologizing for, but I kidded him along to find out what was going on. He said that when a writer is getting started, it's a good idea to pick out someone well known and write something disagreeable about her. Seems like an odd way to get started on a career, but I guess that side of Hollywood does exist. I've never come up against it, though, thanks to Mom and the studio.

Irvin Cobb, master of ceremonies at the Academy Award dinner in 1935, presented Shirley with a kiss and a special Oscar. The award was created for Shirley for her contribution to motion pictures during 1934, the year which carried her to stardom. Cobb referred to Shirley as "the best present ever dropped by Santa Claus down the Christmas chimney of the world."

Shirley's meteoric rise to stardom resulted in a huge demand for publicity "stills." Here are some of the pictures released by the studio publicity mills to satisfy the avid interest of millions.

Stardom does not affect the rank of children in childhood's hierarchy of age, and Shirley, as the youngest of her neighborhood gang, brought up the rear in this informal sidewalk procession. Until constant precautions became necessary to protect her from

any danger, Shirley played with her friends on the streets of Santa Monica as she had always done. Later, the Fox studio insisted that an armed guard be with her at all times, and Shirley's friends came to play with her on the fenced-in grounds of a larger house.

When she was not working on a picture, Shirley was outdoors in the sun most of the time. The entire Temple family often spent Sundays on the beach at Santa Monica. On the opposite page are interior and exterior views of the Santa Monica house into which the Temples moved when they left the five-room bungalow where Shirley passed her babyhood. This house, too, proved inadequate

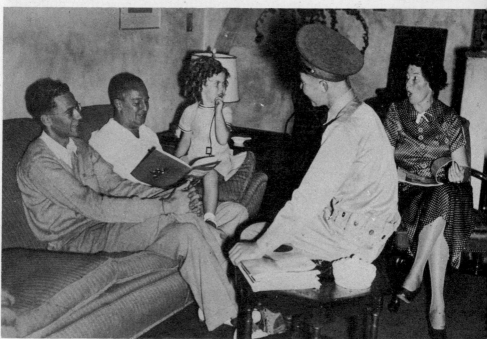

for the comfort and protection of the nation's top star, and a year later the Temples moved again. The bottom picture of a typical family evening shows George Temple, Jr., in the uniform of his military academy. Jack Temple sits at the left, next to his father, who is reading aloud to the family.

79

Though Shirley enjoyed guns and slingshots more than dolls, pictures like this were considered more suitable for publicity release.

In the gardens on the Fox lot, Shirley romps with Buck, a star in his own right, who played in a series of Fox productions. Shirley's passion for animals has always been one of her strongest traits.

Behind the new Santa Monica house, the Temples put up a giant slide for Shirley. Later, when the Temples moved to Brentwood, she had an entire playground of her own.

Shirley used to swing in front of her bungalow between "takes" on *The Stowaway*.

CHAPTER 4

Being a Star

After *Little Miss Marker,* the next picture I made was *Baby Take a Bow,* for Fox. The studio picked the title to remind people of my song with Jimmy Dunn, in *Stand Up and Cheer.* I was a starred player in *Baby,* as we called it, and also in *Now and Forever,* for which Fox loaned me to Paramount again. Then I was starred again in *Bright Eyes.*

When I became a star, Mom and Daddy weren't quite able to keep up their resolution of living exactly the way they'd lived before, because it just wasn't practical. Mom had to get more help because our work took up so much of her time every day. And we had to move for the second time, out of Santa Monica into Brentwood, which is practically the country. That was partly because so many people kept bringing their children to see me that we didn't have much private life, and they thought I'd be better off in a place like Brentwood, where there would be grounds big enough for me to play in, with a strong stone wall around them.

The Brentwood house, where we're still living, is one I really love. There's a nice swimming pool down the hill, and a riding ring for me, and a patio. There's a little playhouse in the yard for me, too—the first house ever made of glass brick. A glass brick manufacturing firm built it for us, on condition that they could use pictures of it in their catalogue. Confidentially, I got the best end of the arrangement.

While the Brentwood house was being built, Mom and I used to go out there every once in a while to check up on how it was coming along. One day, while Mom was talking to the workmen, I poked around and found some nice wet sand and cement by the roadside and started making sand pies. Every time a car would go by, I'd yell, "Nice pies for sale!"

Finally a big car stopped, the driver being a rather astonished director of mine at Fox, Mr. Irving Cummings. I went over to the car, very dead-pan, and asked if he wanted some nice fresh pies, and he dead-panned back and asked how much they were, and I told him two for five. So he gave me a nickel and I offered him one of the nice, sandy pies. He took a look at it and asked me to keep it for him.

My next customer was a tourist who did a double take when she saw me but when she recovered, ordered a pie to send to her niece in Detroit. I told her it might get squashed en route, but the lady said, "Oh, that's all right, dearie. I'll just put it in a bottle."

Then some other cars stopped, and I made more sales. When Mom came back, I'd earned 67 cents, which I showed her with great pride. She wasn't especially pleased, I guess, but she let me keep the money, in memory of my first hard work.

Another thing that happened as a result of my being a star was that I ruined my father's banking business. I really did. It was because of all the mothers and fathers who used to bring their little girls into the bank to see him. He couldn't fight them off. They'd say, "Now listen to how much better my daughter can sing than Shirley!" and the little girl would sing or recite, and then the mother would ask Daddy to get her daughter into the movies. I can't imagine why they thought Daddy would be so delighted if some other little girl turned up and sang better than I did, but there were so many of them that the bank just didn't seem like a bank any more, so Daddy quit and became a business and investment counsellor.

I think the reason so many mothers wanted their children to get into pictures and play the kind of parts I played was that my roles were so often typical of just the things any little girl does at home. That made the mothers feel that their daughters could be stars, too, and I wouldn't be surprised if they were right, because, after all, getting to be a star is partly a matter of chance. I just happened to get there first. But the mothers never seemed to realize that a child of another type would have had a better chance in pictures than a child with hair and clothes and personality just like mine. That's life!

Once Fox decided that it wanted a publicity picture of lots of mothers bringing their little girls to the studio to see if they could be stars too. It sent out a call for them, explaining that the children weren't going to be given a screen test or anything, but the studio just wanted the mothers to line up at the gate and hold their daughters. A perfect mob turned out—hundreds and hundreds of mothers, every one with a curly-headed little girl.

Something else that happened after I became a star was the psychologists. They wanted to find out whether my movie career made me different from other children, and they decided to give me intelligence tests. I remember one Swedish psychologist especially, with a tremendous beard. He was so dignified I didn't dare ask him to let me braid it, but every time he was around I thought about how much fun it would be, so I guess that was what he'd have called a suppressed desire.

He kept asking me questions. He asked me what kind of fish I'd be if I were a fish, and what kind of bird I'd be if I were a bird. I said I'd like to be a pelican and a dolphin, though I actually didn't know what a dolphin was, and I never did find out what that proved about my intelligence. Then he played my favorite game with me, which consisted of drawing a lot of dots and trying to connect them into squares, and I beat him. I guess my staring at his beard made him nervous.

One of Mom's biggest scares came the night we went to the 1935 Academy Award dinner. We were all milling around before we sat down, and my parents were talking to various celebrities. Mom thought I was with Daddy and he thought I was with Mom. Actually, I was roaming around by myself saying hello to everybody and having a grand whirl.

Well, there was a photographer there, one of the oldest free-lancers in the business, who was used to doing whatever he liked, and he held out his hand to me and said, "Come on, Shirley, I want to make some pictures of you."

Of course I knew him but I didn't know he planned to photograph me without studio permission. We disappeared momentarily, just as Mom suddenly turned around and saw I wasn't with Daddy.

Then there was a stupendous hullabaloo. Just about this time Daddy had been getting extortion notes from some poor silly youngster who thought he could scare Daddy into dropping money on his head from an airplane. So naturally the first thing everybody thought was that I'd been kidnapped. They didn't realize that at my ripe old age, I could take care of myself! Well, almost.

People started running all over the hotel and waving their arms and shouting and at last somebody remembered seeing me go out the door with the photographer, and they came downstairs and found us. The photographer got a terrific lecture and the Fox people wouldn't let him enter their studio again for a year.

Then we all sat down, and I sat at the head table with Irvin S. Cobb, who was toastmaster, and Bette Davis, who won the award that year for the best actress. I was only about 6, and I got sleepy pretty early, and wanted awfully to go home, but I had to stay because I was getting a special award for having made the biggest contribution to the movies during the past year.

Mom gave me a big French roll to play with, and I amused myself for a while tearing out its soft insides and making little pellets. I considered throwing them at people, which I certainly would have done if I'd been on the Fox lot, but it didn't seem the right time or place. Another suppressed desire. Finally Irvin Cobb introduced me and gave me my award, and I was so sleepy I could barely stand up on my chair and speak into the mike to thank people for clapping. As soon as we got into the car I fell asleep, and Mom got me into bed without my ever waking. I guess there never was any danger of my getting overtired by making movies, because I was a very direct character, and when I got tired, I simply fell asleep. A nasty habit which I have not yet conquered.

Actually, though, Mom and the studio watched my health as if I'd been a prize fighter in training. Whether it was the care I got or whether I'm just naturally tough I don't know, but I haven't been sick for a total of over 10 days in my whole life, and then it's only been little things like a cold. My time was always planned for me very carefully, but everything was done as if it were a game, and so

I never realized how full the days were.

Every single week day of the school year, I had to spend a certain amount of time studying. That's a California law. The state is very strict about motion-picture children, who must get exactly the same education as children who go to public schools. The studio pays the teachers, but the program is supervised by the Board of Education. Every child has to put in three hours of school work a day, right on the set, and if school work gets behind, picture-making just has to stop until those three hours are finished.

Movie children can't work overtime, either. Everybody at Fox was anxious to work on my pictures, but I suspect these rules had more to do with it than my fatal charm. Nobody had to work over-time, and quite often the director would let the whole cast go home when I did, at 5 o'clock. If the director couldn't fix things so that the adult actors could be used during my school hours, everybody would get time off while I was learning to read "This is a dog" or practicing big round copybook "O's." Board of Education rules just don't reckon with production costs. Lots of times I bet the studio wished I really was a midget, as the English story had it, so they wouldn't have had to worry about getting me educated.

Saturday was my big day, of course, because I always had lots of extra time when I didn't have to study. I'd turn up in the morning just brimming with ideas for things I wanted to do. I'd have doll dresses I wanted Ande, the wardrobe mistress, to cut out for me, and stories I wanted my teacher to tell me, and games to play with everybody. By Saturday night, I guess everybody who worked on the picture was tired enough to be ready for the weekend.

Because I had to spend so much time on school work, from my sixth birthday on, it was especially important for me to have a stand-in. The stand-in takes your place before the camera while they're figuring out lighting and camera angles, which often takes more time than shooting the scene. A double, who takes your place in dangerous scenes requiring athletic skill, has to look pretty much like you, but a stand-in just has to be the same size and have the same color hair and clothes.

For some of my earliest pictures my stand-in was a very cute little girl with bangs, named Marilyn Granas, but for most of them it's been Mary Lou Isleib. Mary Lou's family and mine have been old friends for years, ever since our fathers became acquainted while they were·slaving away in the same bank, and when I needed a stand-in, Mom suggested Mary Lou. That was fun, because Mary Lou and I played together on the set as we had always played together at home, while Mom and Mrs. Isleib sat on the side lines and discussed the problems of parenthood.

Mary Lou and I had a divine time playing and discussing parents, but we weren't able to study together because we had to be in front of the camera at exactly opposite times, so I did my lessons alone with the teacher. Most of the time while I was at Fox my teacher was Miss Frances Klampt, hereafter known as "Klammie," which is what I always called her.

Klammie realized that I lacked some stimulation in school because I didn't have anyone to compete with, so she invented a game in which she herself was my competitor. She pretended that she was another pupil, a droop of a girl named Mergetroid who was barely able to read and write. She'd write something on the blackboard in a bad, sprawly hand and I'd take pride in showing how much better I could do it. Or she'd ask a question in her role as teacher and then she'd quickly switch around and be Mergetroid, and scratch her head and look puzzled while I gleefully raised my hand and shouted "I know!" Both Klammie and I managed to keep the two sides of her dual personality straight, and we had lots of fun with Mergetroid.

While I was making pictures, Klammie and I worked in a little portable house which was a combination dressing room and schoolroom. When I wasn't making a picture, Mom and I showed up at the studio every day just the same, on the dot of nine. Right after breakfast we'd whip off in the car, driven by Grif, and we'd spend the day in the special bungalow which Mr. Sheehan gave me.

The bungalow was part of the Fox "Keep-Temple-Unspoiled" campaign. It was supposed to provide me with a normal environment, and it was as cute as could be. A real little house, off at one corner of the Fox lot, painted white, with a scalloped design around it, and a big blue polka dot right in the middle of every scallop. There was a garden, with a picket fence around it, and a tree with a swing, and a pen for the white rabbits Mr. Sheehan had given me. The rabbits were sort of a problem because of the way they accumulated. There were only two at first, and 11 when we went off on our first trip to Hawaii, and 43 when we got back. Needless to say, the Fox café had "chicken" every day for over a month.

Once I decided to present a rabbit to Mr. David Butler, one of my directors, as a sign of affection. He couldn't quite see how he'd find any use for a white rabbit, but he wanted to get out of it gracefully, so he explained that it would be unfair to the rabbit if he accepted, because one rabbit would get lonesome by itself. In vain I tried to explain that if you had one rabbit you always had lots more after a while. He didn't seem to understand and I had to keep the rabbit myself.

Besides the rabbits, there were a bantam rooster and hen in the back yard, and if I wasn't making a picture, I'd feed the rabbits and chicks myself. The hen naturally laid bantam eggs, and we'd take an egg home every night so that our housekeeper, Katie, could fix it for my breakfast in the morning. This was Mom's stratagem to overcome my negative attitude toward eggs. Every once in a while some of the chicks would get out of their pen, we never knew how, and run around the driveways squawking until a prop man or somebody rounded them up and took them back to the yard. I'm sorry to say that the unrestrained and joyful crowing of my bantam rooster spoiled many movie companies' outdoor shooting. Imagine a movie hero making mad love to a beautiful actress, only to be crowed at!

Inside, the bungalow had a living room done in cherry red, with a white desk and the tiny white piano Mr. Sheehan had given me when I finished *The Little Colonel*. The bedroom, where I was supposed to take a dreary little nap every afternoon until I was seven, had a blue ceiling with silver stars. There was a kitchen, too, and most days Mom and my teacher and I had lunch there, except when we had special guests. Then we'd eat in a separate dining room at the Fox café. The café served yellow tomato juice, which startled me at first, but for which I developed a great passion.

What with the bungalow, and Klammie's knack of making school seem like fun, and all my pals on the Fox lot, I really felt as if I were going home from a party when we had to leave the studio. By the time we were halfway home, though, I'd be thinking about seeing Daddy and the boys again, and it was fun to get home. We'd all have supper together, and then I'd romp awhile with Daddy and my brothers. Then, the very last thing before I fell asleep, Mom would teach me my lines for the next day, and in the morning I'd know them. I guess they sank into my brain while I was sleeping.

The way I knew my lines was always supposed to be remarkable, but I still can't see why. Children often have better memories than grownups because their minds aren't weighted down with a lot of facts and figures. I did develop one trouble, though, as a result of memorizing the dialogue for so many movies. In self-defense I had to get the habit of throwing away what I learned in one picture to be ready for the next. Otherwise my head would have been just crammed with useless chatter, like a messed-up bureau drawer. But when I started going to Westlake and taking examinations, I found that I was pulling the same trick I'd learned in pictures. The minute I passed my exam, I'd forget everything I knew. So I've been trying to develop two kinds of memory, one permanent and one temporary, and the last few years I've done a little better.

While Mom was teaching me the lines, she gave me the right emphasis and intonations. Mr. Irving Cummings, one of the directors, used to say that Mom could have been an actress, because she had an instinctive feeling about how lines should be delivered.

Usually I learned the whole scene, not just my own part, because it made better sense when everything fitted together. The directors sometimes had to warn me not to mouth the words the grownups were saying, and quite often I'd tease the other actors by correcting them if they blew their lines or made mistakes.

Arthur Treacher was the man who figured out how to stop me when I corrected him on dialogue. The second he made a mistake, while I was still drawing breath to correct him, he'd turn on me and roar, "Vile child, you have made a serious error! You are costing this company untold sums of money!" He wasn't really trying to blame me, of course, it was just his way of acknowledging his mistake, but it always tickled me so much I couldn't get around to correcting him.

Lionel Barrymore was very dramatic about the same thing. When he was playing my grandfather in *The Little Colonel,* I told him a line he'd forgotten and he stared at me and said with great intensity, "Thirty years in show business, and now I stand rightfully corrected by a mere moppet!" Actually, I think he got a bang out of it.

Acting was always so real to me that I never had any trouble with crying scenes. Sometimes they blow mentholatum vapor in actresses' eyes to help them cry, but they never did that with me. I'd just go off to one side of the set by myself, so I'd feel lonesome, and pretty soon Mom would come over and talk to me a little, and the tears would flow right along. I could stop them on schedule, too, and go right back to weaving paper mats or whatever else I'd been doing.

Once, though, I started crying and couldn't stop. It was in *The Littlest Rebel*, the scene where I persuaded Abraham Lincoln to pardon my Southern father and the Yankee officer who'd befriended him. It was a tricky scene, because I had to balance between tears and laughter, and I also had to keep eating pieces of an apple which Lincoln was slicing. Some people still think that was the best scene I ever did, and some of the crew cried while it was being shot. Anyhow, I got so worked up that when the scene was over, I couldn't stop crying, and the director had to send me to my dressing room for a little rest. In *The Little Princess* I had to cry when my father didn't recognize me because of amnesia. To start me off they played some sad music on a phonograph, but it only made me laugh. I told them they couldn't get to me that way, because I didn't have any sad memories. So I used the old technique of going off by myself and feeling lonesome, and sure enough, it worked.

One special problem about me was my teeth. Fortunately, my baby teeth fell out one at a time. If a tooth came out in the middle of a picture the dentist would put a tiny porcelain tooth on a little plate that would fit in my mouth. When my own tooth would grow halfway the dentist would then make a porcelain facing that would be held on to my tooth with dental powder. But Mom believed in being prepared, and all the years I was at Fox, she kept a small box in her pocketbook, with two or three spare teeth and some dental powder, for emergencies.

Her patience really broke the night I was to put my footprints in the cement at Grauman's Chinese Theater. On the way to the theater while I worried about how I was going to pull my foot out of the cement after the ceremony, another tooth fell out.

We combed the car for it and finally Mom told me I would just have to keep my mouth closed for the cameraman. So there I was at the biggest moment of my life, a complete deadpan. Not even the giant flashbulbs could surprise a smile out of me.

I used to keep my tooth in a glass of water while I ate so it would be safe. The system seemed foolproof until we went on location at Lake Sherwood. I guess I was too excited to worry about my tooth—at least not until we got home and Mom noticed the gap. I had an early call at the studio the next day so there was nothing for us to do but send a prop man back to the lake with a flashlight. The glass of water had been thrown out, of course, but the prop man brought back the tooth and the show went on.

Shirley finds her ringlets rather hard to manage. Mrs. Temple always supervised Shirley's "make-up" which was negligible except for the curls which had to be carefully combed by Mrs. Temple.

Back view of Shirley's internationally-known coiffure. There were
56 curls. Every night, Mrs. Temple combed Shirley's hair with
water and pinned it up. Once the coiffure was combed out in the
morning, every effort was made to keep it from getting mussed,
because recombing was a lengthy process. Despite the endless
trouble required for this hairdress, there were probably a million

mothers in the United States who arranged their children's hair in the same way, whether it was becoming or not. Shirley's contract with Fox had a provision that nobody except her mother should touch her hair, and she never had the services of a hairdresser until she played in *Kathleen*. Above is the impish, pursed-mouth look which was one of Shirley's most famous expressions.

Photographers considered Shirley a miracle child who was almost incapable of an awkward pose or an unattractive expression. Nothing about Shirley, even close-ups of her hands and feet, lacked

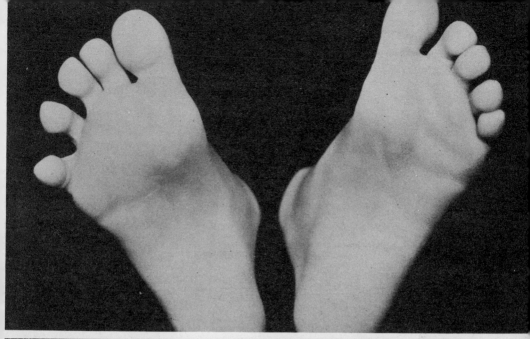

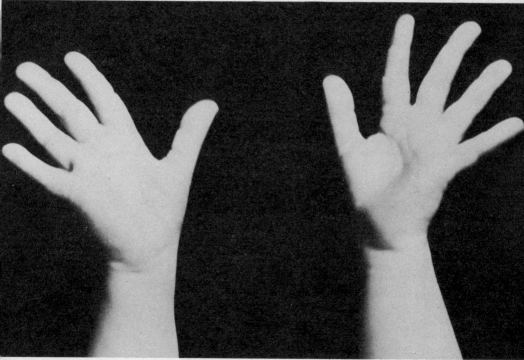

interest for Temple fans. Magazines published interviews with palmists who observed marks of artistic talent in her hands, and writers pointed out the slightly spread toes of her right foot.

When this picture was taken of Shirley's bedroom at home, her doll collection was still small enough to be kept in one room. Later it

grew so large that it was housed in a special chamber lined with air-conditioned glass cases. Eventually a museum will receive it.

This series of stills is from *Curly Top,* a film she starred in with John Boles. Although she was actually only 6, Shirley's song, "When I Grow Up," took her through various stages of her future life. Above, at right, costumed as a debutante, she sang "When I am sweet sixteen I'm going to a ball—Of all the ladies there I'd like to be the best of all—I'll wear a dress of silver and lace, they'll call me Princess Curly—I'll be like Cinderella, 'cept I won't run home so early."

Left, dressed as a bride, Shirley delivered the second verse: "When I am twenty-one I wish that I could look—Like the picture that I saw in a pretty story book—A lady all dressed up in white with flowers in her hand—And such a veil I never saw, the biggest in the land." For a smash finish, she gave her celebrated old-lady routine. "When I get very, very old I'll stay at home all day—But I haven't quite made up my mind, it's much too far away!"*

Like American children everywhere, then as now, Shirley played
one old cat with her friends, but she preferred a badminton racket
to a baseball bat. This photograph was taken at Palm Springs,

102

where Shirley went with her parents for a short vacation every time she finished a picture. Her school work was not interrupted, for her teacher accompanied the Temple family.

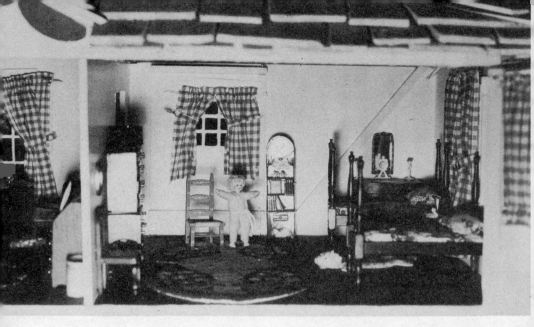

Bedroom of dollhouse used in *Curly Top*, which was afterwards presented to Shirley for her collection of toys.

Bill Robinson riding with Shirley on the miniature car he gave her. It ran by a washing-machine motor, had a governor which kept its speed down to eight miles an hour.

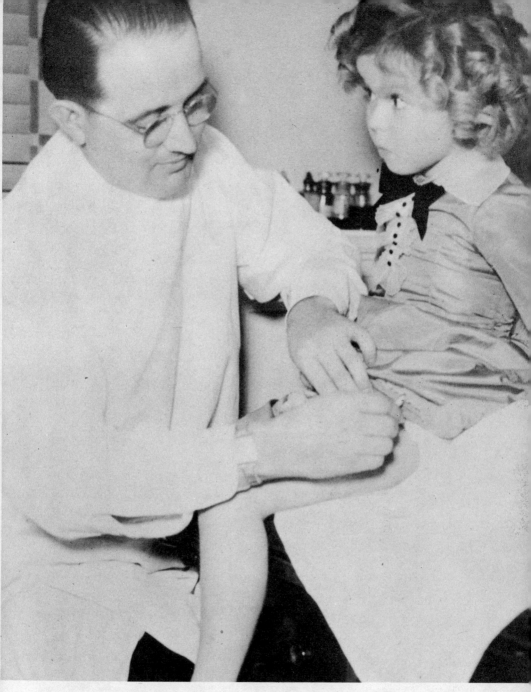

Shirley's health regimen, overseen by her mother, included plenty of sleep, outdoor play, proper diet, and regular medical checkups. The physician who cared for Shirley in her babyhood, and still does, is Dr. Russell Sands, shown here vaccinating Shirley.

This publicity picture was shot at Palm Springs to assure worried fans that Shirley led a normal life with plenty of time to play.

CHAPTER 5

Places and People

When you're a movie star, you meet some of the nicest and most interesting people in the country. That's one of the best things about this life. Some of them came to the studio, and others we visited, and every time I met anyone especially interesting, I got his signature for my autograph album.

When I met General Pershing I naturally wanted his autograph. We had loads of fun looking through my autograph book and I was amazed at how few celebrities in Hollywood he knew. I guess he was too busy being a general. When I was that age people didn't impress me very much, because I hadn't learned to distinguish celebrities and personalities from anyone else. But meeting General Pershing really thrilled me, and I think he was magnificent.

I have the signatures of President and Mrs. Franklin Delano Roosevelt, too. I got Mrs. Roosevelt's first. She was in Hollywood while I was making *Dimples,* and she came to the studio. She watched us rehearse and shoot a scene, and then she and I sat down in a pew that was there for a church scene, and had a talk. She was especially interested in my school work. I showed her my notebook and she was delighted to find that I was studying just the same things as any other child my age. In 1938 I saw her again when I visited at the White House and met President Roosevelt.

I was having a press interview at our hotel in Washington when Mom burst into the room to tell me the President had invited us to the White House. Too excited to eat, and too scared to because one of my wobbly teeth might fall out before the big moment, I finally gave in and had a sandwich. The expected happened and my glamour evaporated in the form of a front tooth. We had to leave immediately to meet the President so nothing could be done to fix me up. As we walked through the White House doors I was completely awed but each step nearer to the President's office made me feel more at home. When I actually came face to face with him I was completely at ease. The President grinned warmly as he shook hands with me but unfortunately I couldn't smile back. He looked a little puzzled and asked me if I was afraid or nervous. I had to tell him the bitter truth about my missing tooth. He rocked back in his chair and chuckled the way I always imagined Santa Claus would chuckle. Then he confided he was missing quite a few himself. After reassuring me that the gaps wouldn't make any difference in the long run, we both had a big laugh and then he signed under his wife's name in my autograph book. I'll always remember the broad grin still on his face as I left the room.

Henry Morgenthau was a pal, too. The first time I met him was quite soon after Roosevelt's first cabinet took office, and I asked Daddy what to say. Daddy suggested that I ask him if he was going to balance the budget, so I did, and he told me very seriously that he was, but I guess he couldn't quite foresee how it was going to work out. Maybe I helped upset the budget, because when we were in Washington he gave me shiny new coins of his own, just minted, of every denomination. I still have them.

There was a constant procession of visitors at the Fox studio. Harry Lauder came and brought me some kilts. John McCormack brought me a book about leprechauns and told me about his grandchildren in Ireland. Rosa Ponselle gave a party for me, and we sang for each other. I became quite attached to her fox terrier who chimed in with us. He used to sit on the piano bench and howl like a banshee whenever Miss Ponselle sang. And an Indian potentate's wife visited me. She had a caste mark on her forehead and a diamond in her nose. I could hardly take my eyes off her.

And then, of course, I met lots of wonderful people just in the course of the picture business. The one who made the first really big impression on me was Jimmy Dunn, as I've said before. He was widely celebrated as my first great love, and I did think he was dreamy. Every other girl in Hollywood did too, and I had a hard time keeping my jealousy under control. Jimmy lived near us before we moved out of Santa Monica, and he used to come over evenings and romp with me. My favorite sport was having Jimmy throw me up in the air and catch me, and I never got tired of it, but Jimmy got very tired indeed.

Once I explained to him that since I weighed only 43 pounds it shouldn't wear him out, but he explained if you tossed 43 pounds in the air 10 times that made 430 pounds, so no wonder he couldn't take it indefinitely.

Jimmy gave me some luscious presents. When I was 5 he gave me my first wrist watch. Mom thought I was too young for a real time-keeper, but Jimmy outguessed her. And on my seventh birthday, he gave me flowers arranged like a wishing-well, and in the bottom of the well was a gold chain with eight letters hanging from it, spelling out "I Love You."

I'll never forget the time Jimmy had to make a parachute jump with me in his arms. The jump was only 5 or 6 feet, but Jimmy almost had a nervous breakdown for fear I'd get hurt. I had to think more about calming Jimmy down than about doing the right things for the camera. Jimmy's wonderful. I don't know of anything that's ever pleased me more than his big comeback in *A Tree Grows in Brooklyn,* and I hope he stars in a hundred more pictures.

Gary Cooper was another big crush. One of the first important pictures I made was *Now and Forever,* for which Fox loaned me to Paramount. Gary and Carole Lombard were in it, and we had quite a time. At first Gary scared me because he seemed so awfully tall, but I got over that when he started teaching me to draw. He called me "Wigglebritches" because I never sat still.

Carole Lombard was lovely. I used to pretend to be her director, and I'd shout, "Now don't mumble," and she'd mumble and mug like mad. I was so grieved when Carole was killed in that plane crash on her War Bond tour. She was a real war heroine, I think.

Traveling is the only way to meet all kinds of people, and I'm always more interested in that than in the scenery. Considering my age, I've been able to do quite a lot of traveling. The three trips we've made to Hawaii were the best. I'm actually insane about Hawaii. The first time we got on that big boat I was so excited I nearly popped, and I've been hardly less excited on other trips.

It's definitely thrilling to go to sleep in a stateroom and know that while you're sleeping, the boat is taking you closer and closer to Hawaii. The captain took me up to the bridge, and generally gave me the run of the ship. He usually let me hold the wheel at least once a trip.

Then the boat gets in, and there's a band playing on the dock, and everybody heaps you with flower leis. And the scenery is so beautiful. It's the way a movie set looks when you see it on the screen—not like it looks when you're working on it. After the war, I want to go to Hawaii again. Maybe it has honeymoon possibilities.

On our last trip to Hawaii we lived in a house on the far side of the island and the thing I remember best about that trip was the baseball team I played on. It was a regular League of Nations in miniature. There must have been 40 or 50 kids on it, including two American boys, a Filipino boy, a Chinese boy, a little English girl and me. When we visited an aquarium I was petrified by an octopus in a glass tank, which spat ink at me when I went up close to look at it. Of course the ink couldn't reach me, but I got quite a start.

We tried to avoid publicity as much as possible on these trips, but usually there were so many people who had enjoyed my pictures and wanted to see me that I had to make one public appearance. Mom says that the first time I was in Hawaii people were coming from all over the surrounding country to see me so the government officials finally asked her if I would sing for them. I appeared on the four lanais of Princess Liliuokalani's Palace and sang "The Good Ship Lollipop" through a microphone. There were so many people there that I had to sing it in four directions, four times. Somebody told me there were 40,000 people. All I could see was a lot of faces stretching out in every direction. When they clapped, it was like a thunderstorm coming up. I was glad when it was over.

In 1936 we made a grand trip to Canada. We traveled by car. Grif had to come along, of course, and Doc Bishop of Fox came to worry about any business matters that might come up. He went on most of our trips, which was a great advantage to me because he was always ready to teach me golf or tennis or hold me up while I experimented riding a bicycle.

We reached Seattle on a Sunday and found there was a convention at the hotel. I think it was the Catholic Charities. The chairman came up to our room to ask if I wouldn't like to be an honorary delegate and come downstairs to the ballroom where they were meeting to receive badges. I always liked to get badges, so I agreed, and Mom and Doc and I went down to the meeting and I had my badge pinned on and was ready to go away.

But, instead, the chairman took me up on the stage before about 500 people and asked me to say something. I saw Mom and Daddy looking panicky, because nobody had known this was going to happen, but I figured it was always safe to say thank you, so I said it, and they clapped. This didn't seem to be quite enough, so I said I was glad to be there and hoped they'd have a good convention, and blew them a kiss and said good-bye. When I got down from the platform, Doc wiped his forehead with his handkerchief and said, "Shirley, from now on you can give your own speeches right off the cuff; you don't need any advice from me."

Mom's idea of a quiet trip didn't work out so well. There were so many people who wanted to see us that we couldn't get out of our Seattle hotel. Three thousand people were waiting while we were in the dining room and the manager suggested that we go up to our room by a side door, but Mom never liked to do that. She always hoped that people wouldn't know we were there, but if they found out about it and came to see us, she thought the least we could do was to repay their interest by waving hello.

So the hotel people formed a kind of flying wedge around us, and Daddy put me on his shoulders, and we went through the lobby. Just before we got to the elevators, one little girl came up with a tiny celluloid doll for me. The doll was nude, and I remember thinking how cold it must be. So as soon as we got to our rooms I ran to the little suitcase that I was allowed to take on trips, filled with any silly thing that I wanted to bring with me, and I took out some laces and ribbons given me by Ande, and began making a dress for the doll.

Doc Bishop saw me sitting there on the floor dressing the doll, and he whispered to Mom and opened the door to the next room, where a lot of reporters and photographers were waiting to interview me. "Gentlemen of the press," he said, "let me introduce you to Miss Temple." They were quite surprised to see me sitting on the floor dressing the doll, because they had expected to find me posed properly in a chair waiting to say proper things and have my picture taken.

In Victoria, we had an even worse time with the crowds. We were leaving the hotel to shop for some new sports clothes for Mom, and we found a solid mass of people in the street. Daddy and I somehow became separated from Mom and Doc Bishop in the melee. By the time they found us the streets were so jammed that traffic had to be rerouted. Finally, the police were called to keep us from being trampled. The police took a rope and made a circle around us, and then they actually started to kick and club people out of the way.

It was terrible. Mom and I almost cried, but finally Daddy got it through the policemen's heads that we thought it was unfair for them to kick people who were friendly and just wanted to see us. Then Daddy put me on his shoulders and carried me to the car, very slowly, so that I could wave to everyone, but when we got to the car I really did have to cry a little.

Victoria was also where I caught my first really big fish. We trolled for two days with a guide named Bill, who ran a fishing launch in the Sound. We'd start out at ten, take a box lunch, and spend the whole day on the water. I didn't get anything until the second day, but then I caught a super-colossal fighting salmon. I reeled it in myself until the very end, when Daddy helped me just a little. It weighed 11 pounds, and the chef at the hotel broiled it for dinner. I was so enthusiastic about eating it that later on the guide, Bill, sent three enormous salmon to Hollywood, frozen in a cake of ice, and I gave a salmon dinner at the Fox café for my friends.

In Victoria, when we got to our hotel room, it was full of beautiful baskets of flowers, and Doc Bishop collected the cards so he could write thank-you notes. One of the loveliest baskets didn't have a card, and Doc had no way of knowing who sent it. Later on he heard that, of all the cards to get lost, it had to be the Lord Mayor's, and the Lord Mayor was greatly hurt because he had sent flowers and we hadn't acknowledged them.

No one wants to offend a Lord Mayor, so when we heard this, we invited him to have dinner with us at the hotel. He was nice, but so dignified that we couldn't quite think what to talk about after we'd said all the polite things. Daddy, leaping into the conversational breach, asked the Lord Mayor how long he'd been in Victoria and the Lord Mayor said austerely, "Thirty-four years."

"Well," said Daddy, "looks like you'll be a permanent resident." I nearly swallowed a bone, it was so hard to keep from laughing, but the Lord Mayor didn't crack a smile.

In 1938, we motored across the country to visit Washington and Boston and New York. This was a kind of "see America first" junket to educate me. We didn't make advance reservations but just stopped for the night wherever we happened to be. One night we stopped at a motor court in Colorado. Daddy asked the man how much it would be and he counted us up and said, "Thirteen dollars, cash in advance, please."

Then he recognized us and got all excited. He took the $13 and said, "I'll be right back," and he came into the little bedroom, where Mom was starting to put me to bed, with towels and great quantities of soap just spilling from his hands. Mom was so impressed she counted, and there were nineteen towels and fifty guest cakes of soap. It wasn't that he thought we were terribly dirty. The gift of extra soap and towels was simply his way of showing us we were welcome.

When we were going through the Midwest, *Life* Magazine wanted a picture of me standing in a Kansas wheatfield. Their photographer met us as we entered the state of Kansas and we found a wheatfield and I had my picture taken and they ran it for a cover. It seemed simple enough, but when the magazine came out, Dad got a letter from a Kansas farmer who claimed it was his wheatfield and he ought to have some money because his wheat had had its picture taken.

He didn't make any pretense of having seen us on his land, and actually we'd been miles away from his place, but he said he recognized his wheat by the way it looked. I don't see how he thought he could identify it, because wheat is wheat. Daddy turned the letter over to *Life,* and they did the arguing.

When we arrived in the East, we saw all the historical places, and picnicked in Hyde Park with Mrs. Roosevelt, visited Governor Lehman, and then we sailed to Bermuda.

Next to Hawaii, I loved Bermuda best. The boat we sailed on was the "Queen of Bermuda" and she really was queen of the line. Never have I seen such a spotless boat. Gertrude Lawrence was on board and until we became good friends, I identified her as the lady with the leopard-skin shoes and lucite purse. The shoes were covered with tiny bells so you could hear her coming and going all over the boat. The bag fascinated me because you could see all the tricky gadgets she carried through it. I wanted one then, but have since decided it would be much too hard to keep everything in order for constant inspection. One night the captain asked us to sit at his table for dinner. When Miss Lawrence came in she kept pushing up her long full sleeves which were in vogue then. In all the innocence of my 9 years I announced to the table at large, "My, that dress doesn't fit you very well, does it?" There was a deadly silence, then Miss Lawrence's famous sense of humor saved the day. When she burst out laughing, the rest of the party did too, and I laughed hardest of all.

When we reached Bermuda I was fascinated by the glass-bottomed boats that you look through to see the fish and seaweed and coral caves under water, and I was especially fascinated by the way you go around by bicycle and horse and buggy instead of by automobile. Just before we left Bermuda I was permitted to sit up with the driver and take the reins. It was loads of fun to drive two big black horses. Little native children would run after our ponies shouting for autographs and pennies. I really believe the pennies were much more attractive to them than an autograph. One little native boy ran for miles, clinging to the side of the cart, telling me the story of a picture I had been in. As if I didn't know it by heart!

When we got back from Bermuda, I got an upset stomach in Boston and had to stay in bed four days, and the London newspapers telephoned every day to see if I was feeling better.

Big trips like that had to be taken in the summertime, when I didn't have any school work, but every time I finished a picture, we'd take a short vacation trip to Palm Springs, or sometimes to Yosemite. Klammie went along and I had my school work as usual and spent the rest of the time outdoors. Once J. Edgar Hoover was at Yosemite when we were, and I played golf with him and some other G-men. I didn't actually play in their foursome, but I had my small clubs and balls and went around the course when they did. It was really something to see them run when I called, "Fore," because, of course, there was absolutely no way to tell in what direction the ball would go when I hit it. They'd just scatter for the nearest cover.

At that time I was Public Menace Number One to J. Edgar Hoover. So much so they finally quarantined me inside of a fence originally built to protect the trees from deer. To make up to me for the insult, Mr. Hoover gave me a china deer and skunk as golf "trophies." When we met again at Arrowhead about a year later, he added two more figures to my collection.

The Temples embark for the first of their three Hawaiian trips.

Shirley's father carries her down the gangplank in Honolulu, to protect her from a mob of fans gathered on the dock. While Shirley was in Hawaii, a delegation of Japanese-descended Hawaiians presented her with a life-sized Japanese bride doll, purchased with pennies contributed by 20,000 Hawaiian-Japanese school children. The doll's value is so great that when it was borrowed for exhibition at a California fair, it was transported in an ambulance.

Other gifts presented to Shirley on her Hawaiian trip included 200 pounds of candy, 43 fans, 3 surfboards, and 18 silk parasols. The enthusiastic natives contributed enough miscellaneous presents to fill half a dozen packing cases.

Twenty thousand people thronged the Honolulu streets to see
Shirley ride by. Armed policemen flanked her on the running
boards in case crowds got out of hand. When she returned to Los
Angeles, 3,000 admirers greeted her at the station.

In her studio bungalow, Shirley played and studied like any other little girl. Here she is coloring a scrapbook.

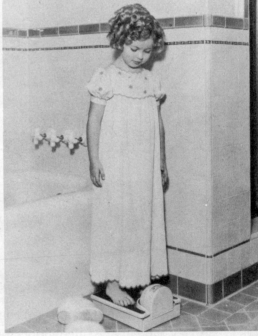

Shirley's fitters inspect the hang of her dress. Right, Shirley weighs in. Like every Hollywood star, she has always watched her weight.

Shirley's bedroom at home was simply done, but filled with the usual little girl's dolls, animals, whatnot shelf and books.

The playhouse on the grounds of the present Temple home was a birthday present to Shirley from a glass manufacturer.

Shirley with Mary Lou Isleib, her friend and stand-in. Mary Lou's father worked with Mr. Temple in the California Bank.

On the set of *Bowery Princess*, Shirley rests and talks to a script girl while the camera crew arrange their lights.

Her first bicycle lesson. Left, "Doc" Bishop, Fox public-relations man who accompanied the Temples on most of their trips. Right, Griffith, the armed guard who, under the terms of Shirley's studio contract, had to go with her everywhere, to protect the greatest financial asset of Fox's $54,000,000 company. Griffith had formerly guarded Darryl Zanuck's children.

Shirley rests halfway up the 50-foot spiral stairway used for the lighthouse scene in *Captain January,* one of Shirley's hardest assignments. She tapped down this stair, reciting the multiplication table.

Released in 1936, *Captain January* smashed box-office records in major cities from coast to coast. Shirley rehearses "The Codfish Ball," hit number of the film.

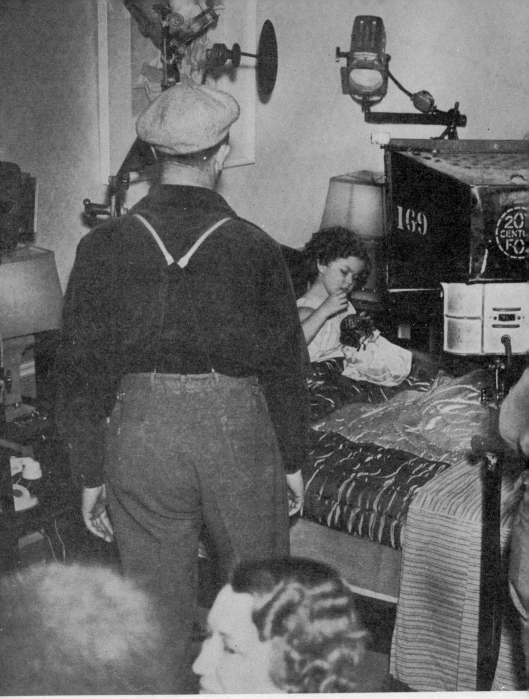

On the set, Shirley plays with a doll while waiting for lights to be adjusted. Mrs. Temple, who was paid a thousand dollars a week for her care of Shirley, was never far off at times like this, although she tried to keep out of the range of the still cameras.

126

Often she caught a misplaced curl or disordered costume which had escaped the director's attention. Shirley can still hear her mother's low tones across a noisy set, still accepts suggestions on the reading of a line or the delivery of a gesture.

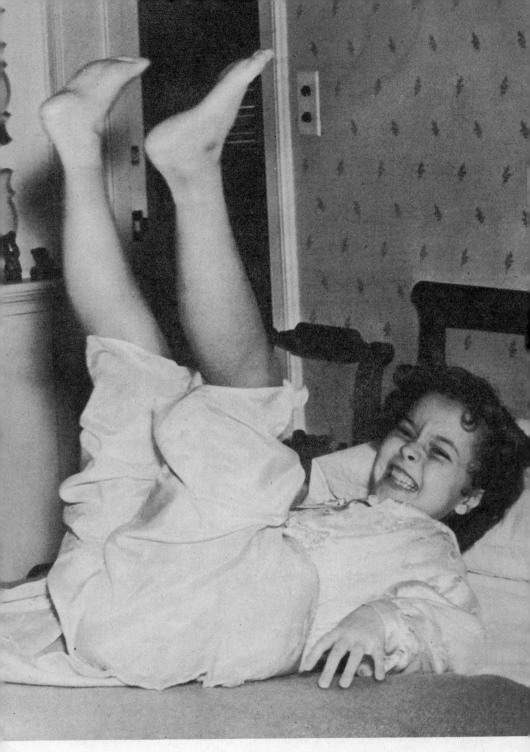

The junior G-woman roughhouses before bedtime.

CHAPTER 6

Tomboy Temple

My tastes in entertainment were strictly blood and thunder. I was practically breathless when Mom let me go to a Western movie, and when it came to radio, *Gang Busters* and the *Lone Ranger* were strictly my dish.

I loved contests and radio fan clubs, too, but I had trouble with them because no one would believe that I was really Shirley Temple. Once I entered a contest for a slogan describing how healthy a certain breakfast food made you, and they wrote me a letter advising me not to pretend I was Shirley Temple, but just to be myself and everybody would like me much better.

After that sad experience, I decided I needed a pen name. One of the radio shows was offering to send children code descriptions of what was going to happen next, with a decoder pin to help you figure it out, so I sent in for the decoder pin under my pen name and everything worked out fine. After that, when the hero was tied to the stake with Apaches yelling around him, I wasn't worried, because I had found out through the code that he was going to escape.

After Klammie and I finished school work, we were constantly sneaking up on each other, pretending that she was a bandit and I was a policewoman. I caught her cracking safes and holding people up and climbing into second-story windows and doing many other things which were not typical of her at all, because she was little and cute, with big brown eyes.

The most marvellous thrill of my life came when J. Edgar Hoover made me a G-woman. He sent me a badge the size of your thumbnail, with all the proper papers to go with it. I had a basket of toy guns and pistols which I liked better than my dolls, and I was a real demon with a slingshot.

My first slingshot was presented to me by Uncle Billy Robinson, the Negro tap dancer, who made what Mom considered a serious error by giving it to me at the studio instead of at home. That meant I had it to play with on the set all day, and it certainly was a miracle I didn't knock anybody out. Then I practiced at home and became really good. It was a priceless break when I actually had to use a slingshot in *The Littlest Rebel,* potting Jack Holt, who played the Yankee captain. John Boles, my Confederate father, remarked that he was glad to be a Southern gen'leman instead of a "damyankee," so he wouldn't have to stand up to that slingshot.

The worst thing I ever did with my slingshot, probably, was to aim it at the back of a chair on the hotel porch where we were staying for a Palm Springs vacation. I didn't think anyone was sitting in the chair, but when my pebble hit it, a bald head popped up above the chair back and an angry-looking red face turned around and yelled at me and I ran like anything. If Mom had found out I would have had to apologize to the man, but I have concealed the crime until this minute and now it is too late.

My taste for cops-and-robbers stuff finally started the Shirley Temple Police Force, which grew to be an enormous thing. It began when I put a paper clip in the lapel of Anthony Ugrin's coat. He was my still photographer; I told him that wearing the clip made him a policeman and I was chief of police.

One of the prop men asked to join the force, so I put a paper clip in his lapel, too, and pretty soon nearly everybody on the set was going around ornamented with paper clips. Then I decided that the director should be chief of police and offered to abdicate, but the director wanted me to retain my high position and joined the ranks instead. Finally the director presented me with a box of little tin badges with the inscription, "Shirley Temple Police Force," painted on in black lettering.

130

First thing every morning I'd line up the Shirley Temple Police Force for inspection and look at their badges. There was a 5-cent fine for people who had forgotten their badges, and a 1-cent fine for not having it polished, and a thumping $5-fine for anyone who had lost a badge or given it away. I made Mrs. Roosevelt a member of the force and fined her $5 for giving her badge to her niece.

I made scads of money on fines, but I didn't keep it. Part of it furnished a Girl Scout room in Santa Monica, another part helped to build a recreation room for boys in a Santa Monica school and the rest went into the Babies Milk Fund. The line-up was quite a ceremony. People who had forgotten their badges were very much embarrassed, and sometimes a man who didn't have his badge would signal to a friend farther up the line, who'd already passed inspection, to pass his badge along behind everybody's backs. Generally I was able to spot this low deception.

Studio visitors usually joined the force. Once some Los Angeles policemen came over to make me an honorary member of the department, so after they'd given me a badge and enrolled me in their force, I gave them badges and enrolled them in mine. J. Edgar Hoover has a Shirley Temple badge, too. When we visited Washington in 1938 we called on him, and there he was sitting at his big desk with my police badge on his lapel. The badge was so dull that he should have had a 1-cent fine, but I didn't have the nerve to impose it.

The badge came in handy once for Mr. Alan Dwan, the director who had the little tin badges made for me. He was zipping along Sunset Boulevard at an illegal rate of speed and a policeman stopped him, so he very nonchalantly opened his coat and flashed his Shirley Temple Police badge and said with aplomb, "This is official." He got away with it, too; maybe because he really deceived the policeman or maybe because the policeman had a sense of humor.

I had two special Shirley Temple Police badges of my own. One was a super-colossal badge made for me at the studio tin shop. It practically covered my whole front. The other was a present from Uncle Billy: a gold badge set with a real diamond. Of course I prized the gold badge because it came from Uncle Billy, who was always one of my favorite friends.

One of the most super presents I ever received was the tiny car

Uncle Billy gave me. When Uncle Billy came on the set one day, pushing the car, with its motor running, I was thrilled pink. They had a great time with me on the set that day. I hardly could stay out of the car long enough to do my scenes. I wouldn't stop driving even for Anthony to take pictures of me at the wheel.

With Uncle Billy perched on the back end, we drove the car all over the set, right over cables and into scenery and almost into cameras and people. At lunch time I wouldn't eat, but drove the car on the studio streets. We took it home at night and I went all over the grounds. Usually I was pretty good about going to bed when told, but that night Mom had to call Daddy to strong-arm me into the house.

All this sounds as if I'd been pretty much of a tomboy, and I was. If Grif hadn't kept his eagle eye on me, I'd probably have been up near the ceiling running along the catwalks. Studios have to be very careful of child players if they're at all adventurous because there's plenty of dandy trouble to get into on a movie lot.

Grif caused one of my life's most shattering disappointments. An elephant had been rented from the Los Angeles zoo for *Wee Willie Winkie*. It was a most amiable animal, and was used to being ridden by children. For a gag shot, Anthony took a picture of the director, John Ford, being picked up in the elephant's trunk while reading the script. The minute I saw the fun Mr. Ford was having I was wild to have the elephant pick me up too. I worked on Mom for days, and I practically had her sold on the idea of allowing it when Grif crossed me up. Since he had authority to forbid anything he thought dangerous, the elephant and I never got together.

Another disappointment happened to me in *Heidi*. There was a scene in which I was supposed to slide down the bannisters and take a thumping fall. I slid down the bannisters all right, in person, but they cut the scene just before I got to the bottom and had a prop man waiting to catch me. In spite of my pleas, they wouldn't let me take my own fall. They had a double, a little boy dressed just like me, with a head full of curls, and he made the crash landing in my place. It was all I could do not to hate him. But I did manage to get a certain amount of excitement legitimately, like tap-dancing down the spiral lighthouse staircase in *Captain January*. It was about 10 times as high as myself, and I'm afraid Mom had some anxious moments, but I loved it.

One time I really did get into trouble—with the roast turkey they used in *Poor Little Rich Girl*. It was a big, beautiful, nicely browned turkey, and from the moment I was introduced to the appetizing bird I had my eye on it. By the time I'd played my scene with it a couple of times, I was drooling. It was a real break for me when Mom left the set for a dentist appointment. The minute she was out of sight I asked Mr. Irving Cummings, who was directing, if I could have the turkey. He said, "I am not looking at you, Miss Temple," and instantly everybody on the set, especially me, leaped upon the turkey. The men cut it up with their pocket-knives and we ate it to the last pinfeather.

I swore everyone to secrecy and Mom knew nothing about the feast until next day, when I woke up with a ghastly stomach-ache and had to stay in bed. Mr. Cummings' remorse was more painful to him, I'm sure, than the stomach-ache was to me. Next time there was a roast turkey in one of my pictures they sprayed it with Flit. They did it to "keep off the flies," but I suspect their purpose was to keep off Shirley Temple. Anyhow, it certainly was a waste of good turkey.

Mr. Cummings was a grand director. When he shot a scene without sound he told everybody on the set to go ahead and talk, which is most unusual because many directors feel that they must have absolute silence to help them concentrate even when they are not recording sound. And he did so many nice things no one ever heard about, like paying the expenses for a sick baby belonging to one of the property men. With me he was very elegant and stately. He'd greet me every morning in his very mellow voice, "Ah, Miss Temple, and how is my star this morning?" I'd keep a straight face and say, "Very well, thank you, Mr. Cummings, and is your health quite fine?" Mr. Cummings became angry with me only once, and then it was mostly my fault. He was telling me how to play a scene. I couldn't really look directly at him because the sun was shining in my eyes. Looking at the sun has always been difficult for me. He said, "Shirley, when I speak to you I want you to look at me, not in another direction. You are being very rude." He then dismissed the company although he hadn't finished the day's work. I knew he was cross at me and I felt very sorry. The next morning I explained that the sun had been in my eyes, and he picked me up and apologized for misunderstanding. I don't think many men would have been big enough to apologize to a little girl, especially since it was more my fault than his. For a reconciliation gift he brought me my first orchids, tiny white ones in a florist's box. He was probably sorry he'd thought of the idea, because I insisted on wearing my corsage all day, and since my costume definitely did not call for an orchid corsage, it had to be pinned on and unpinned constantly.

Going on location was always a special treat, because it meant traveling and eating box lunches. One of my early location trips was when I made *Now and Forever*. We went to Lake Arrowhead, and there I first became a fishing enthusiast.

We did a scene in which I was supposed to be fishing, and I liked it so well I made Mom promise me that I could fish some more after I finished my school work. Late in the afternoon, I went out on a little pier. I no sooner dropped my line in the water than there was a big tug. Sure enough, I pulled up a fish. It must have been all of 7 inches long, but to me it looked like a whale. Of course I wasn't a bit puzzled that such a sleepy little fish could have yanked my line so hard.

I put it in my basket, highly delighted, and dropped my line in again, and bing—another tug and another sleepy fish. As you can see, I was having exceptional luck. What I didn't know was that one of the company men wearing a rubber suit and boots was standing under the pier where I couldn't see him. He had a pail of fish he had caught earlier in the day and he was putting one after another on my line as fast as I could drop it in. I'd have been pretty disillusioned if I'd found out about it then, but nobody told me until it was too late in my life to make any difference.

One of the biggest jokers at the studio was Arthur Treacher, who was in quite a few of my pictures. During this period I couldn't read very well, and I loved to pounce on people and get them to read the funnies to Mary Lou and me. Most people were quite docile, but Arthur Treacher used to make up his own words. He'd get a dead-pan expression and say in a hollow voice, "It says here that Shirley Temple did something FRIGHTFUL today, something perfectly FRIGHTFUL." I'd implore him to tell me what it was, and he'd insist that it was too FRIGHTFUL to mention, and finally he'd inform me that it was known that I'd bitten Mom on the leg, or set fire to the house, or something else equally revolting.

Naturally I missed no opportunity to tease him. Once I caught him asleep in his dressing room. He looked so funny I tiptoed out and asked Anthony Ugrin to take a picture of him. The next morning the first thing he saw as he walked into his dressing room was the picture of the sleeping Mr. Treacher propped up on his make-up table labeled "This Fish Is Extinct."

Poor Mr. Treacher was also the victim of another idea that I never grew tired of. It began when we were working on a picture that had a stable on the set. I decided that Arthur Treacher would make a very fine horse, and I must say he was very co-operative. He had to spend all of his leisure time in the stall, and finally it got to be such a standard arrangement that the electrician fixed a lamp so he could read in there. While he'd be in there reading, I would bring in my friends and introduce him as my horse, and he'd neigh obligingly.

I am sure there is nobody in the world except Arthur Treacher who can neigh with an English accent.

When I got old enough for real horses, or rather for ponies, I was so crazy about them that the family made a special riding ring for me on the grounds of our Brentwood home. My first pony was Spunky, who was given to me by Mr. Joseph Schenck. Spunky was a historical pony, because he came from England on the "Queen Mary's" first trip. That gave the studio a good publicity angle, so they decided to carry the idea a little further and have the pony flown from New York to Hollywood, which would be the first time a pony had been transported by air. But I put my foot down on that idea, because I was afraid the pony would be frightened or hurt.

So the pony came by train, and I went to meet it at the station. I took a lei of flowers with me, because when we went to Hawaii people had greeted us with flowers to make us feel welcome, and I wanted Spunky to feel very welcome. I put the lei around Spunky's neck and gave him his name right away, because I thought it took a lot of spunk for a pony to keep his spirits up on such a trip.

Spunky was nice, but rather peppery. He used to buck and chase

135

the other horses, and it was Spunky rather than Shirley who decided whether or not he was in a mood to be saddled and ridden.

Dogs and horses! They're two of my greatest passions. I couldn't possibly live without a dog around the house. When I was a little girl we had two, a Scotty and a Cocker, and then Doc Bishop gave me Ching, my first miniature Pekinese. Ching was a beautiful little dog, but she was jinxed. She had the very unglamorous habit of eating the wrong things. She ate nails and buttons and fur and pieces of wood, and everything else she could pick up on the set, which was plenty. One day she swallowed a button and then the trouble began. She had to have an operation. That dog spent more than half of her life in the hospital.

Poor Ching, when she was sick every hair in her nice silky tail would droop and her head would go down and I'd feel just as miserable as she did. Ande, the wardrobe mistress, used to say that when Ching was well, everybody felt happy, because I felt the same way Ching did and my spirits affected other people.

Ching played in *Stowaway*, and I got $10 for her screen appearance. Mom never gave me any bigger allowance than she thought would be good for me, so the extra ten bucks came in very handy for Christmas presents.

I had Ching seven years. One day she ran out in the street while the gate was open and was run over and killed by a car. She was so tiny that the driver couldn't see her. I felt terrible about it, but assuring the frantic driver that I wouldn't hold it against him took up so much of my energy that I couldn't do much grieving.

Soon after, I got Ching II, my present dog. She's also a miniature peke and weighs about 5 pounds. I considered trying to get Ching the part of Moronica in *Kiss and Tell*, but I didn't have the heart to cast her for a part with a name like that, so they got a very clever dog to play Moronica, a Kerry Blue. I had fun between scenes making her do tricks.

One of the few times when being in the movies turned out to be a disadvantage was years ago when my black Scotty, Corky, disappeared. It seems Scottish terriers have to run away. I adored Corky and when I couldn't find him anywhere, I worried so much I was almost ill. Mom telephoned the studio and they told her they would ask the newspapers to run an item about the lost dog and offer a reward. But the newspapermen thought it was just another publicity stunt, and an antiquated one at that.

A couple of days went by and Corky didn't come home and I was so worried I could hardly eat. Finally Fox persuaded a radio station to announce that Corky was lost and to give a description of him. A Hollywood correspondent for the London *Daily Express* heard the announcement, cabled London, and around 10 o'clock that night London called us at home asking if Corky had been found.

Every day that Corky was missing, London telephoned and the *Express* ran daily bulletins. Finally Corky came home by himself. He was a very sick and bedraggled pup, and for his adventure had to spend a week in the hospital.

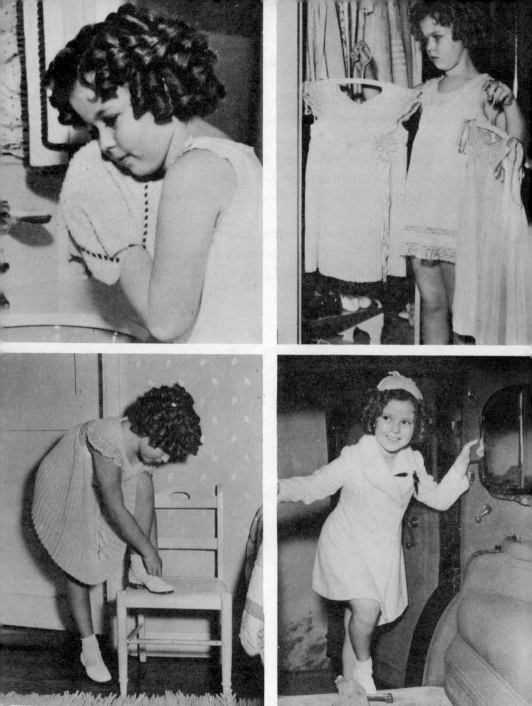

Shirley prepares for the première of *Wee Willie Winkie,* one of the series of "vehicles" in which Fox cast Shirley, which altogether earned the company a grand total of $20,000,000 . . .

. . . and arrives to face a cheering mob and a battery of photographers. Nine years old and in the fourth grade, Shirley had already outpulled every other star at the box office for three years.

At a California fair, Shirley rode on every concession, indulged her love of automobiles . . .

Shirley and her teacher, Klammie, ride the Ferris Wheel. Shirley's guard, Griffith, always came along on such expeditions. The

. . . and horses. She swings around the merry-go-round reaching out to hook a free ring.

Temples received many extortion notes threatening Shirley's kidnapping, but the senders were always tracked down by the FBI.

Shirley greets her pony, Spunky, just arrived from England on the "Queen Mary."

Shirley had her own tennis racket and wielded it vigorously during vacation jaunts.

Left, Mary Lou Isleib and her mother. Right, Bob Ripley visits
Shirley on the studio lot.

Shirley's teacher, Frances Klampt (right), looks on at Shirley's
Chinese lesson. Shirley spoke 400 Chinese words in *Stowaway*.

Shirley Temple.

10-27-37

★

October 28 '36.

cried	kept
cried	kept
cried	kep.t
cried	kept
cried	kept
cried	kept
drank	fur.
drank	fur
drank	fur
drank	fur
drank	fur

Shirley Temple.

fur kept cried drank

Samples of Shirley's school work. Studio teachers kept her abreast of other children her age, enabled her to enter Westlake School in the seventh grade with girls who averaged a year older than herself. Shirley's I.Q. of 150 is thought to denote genius, and psycholo-

144

Shirley Temple.

Shirley Temple
10-27-37

November 13, 1936

$$
\begin{array}{r}
2 \\
62 \\
83 \\
47 \\
+39 \\
\hline 231
\end{array}
\qquad
\begin{array}{r}
1 \\
61 \\
93 \\
26 \\
+19 \\
\hline 199
\end{array}
\qquad
\begin{array}{r}
2 \\
71 \\
58 \\
8 \\
+76 \\
\hline 213
\end{array}
\qquad
\begin{array}{r}
1 \\
62 \\
15 \\
76 \\
+84 \\
\hline 237
\end{array}
$$

$$
\begin{array}{r}
2 \\
28 \\
29 \\
+93 \\
\hline 150
\end{array}
\qquad
\begin{array}{r}
48 \\
63 \\
+67 \\
\hline 178
\end{array}
\qquad
\begin{array}{r}
69 \\
93 \\
+14 \\
\hline 166
\end{array}
\qquad
\begin{array}{r}
97 \\
29 \\
+78 \\
\hline 204
\end{array}
$$

$$
\begin{array}{r}
76 \\
-45 \\
\hline 31
\end{array}
\qquad
\begin{array}{r}
59 \\
-20 \\
\hline 39
\end{array}
\qquad
\begin{array}{r}
108 \\
-65 \\
\hline 43
\end{array}
\qquad
\begin{array}{r}
68 \\
-32 \\
\hline 36
\end{array}
$$

$$
\begin{array}{r}
98 \\
-61 \\
\hline 37
\end{array}
\qquad
\begin{array}{r}
61 \\
-20 \\
\hline 41
\end{array}
\qquad
\begin{array}{r}
147 \\
-87 \\
\hline 60
\end{array}
\qquad
\begin{array}{r}
84 \\
-31 \\
\hline 53
\end{array}
$$

$$
\begin{array}{r}
75 \\
-48 \\
\hline 33
\end{array}
\qquad
\begin{array}{r}
49 \\
-9 \\
\hline 40
\end{array}
\qquad
\begin{array}{r}
29 \\
-6 \\
\hline 23
\end{array}
\qquad
\begin{array}{r}
47 \\
-20 \\
\hline 27
\end{array}
$$

gists who talked with Shirley found her exceptionally brilliant. However, her intelligence expressed itself in her acting, her phenomenal ability to learn lines, and her knack for getting along with people rather than in unusual scholastic achievements.

Shirley learned to swim at an early age. She began by practicing strokes near a Hollywood pool.

At Palm Springs, Shirley clowns for a friend's camera. She has always possessed a strong sense of comedy.

With Hulda Anderson, wardrobe mistress for Shirley's pictures. Later Shirley tells how she promoted "Ande's" romance.

Upper left, Mrs. Temple coaches Shirley for the scenes shown in the following pictures. Shirley dances with a dummy in *Stowaway*, guides him to a bench as the cameras close in.

On her second trip to Hawaii, Shirley realized one of childhood's dreams by being allowed to take the wheel of a great ship. Captain Johnson of the "Matsonia" watches his new skipper confidently.

Two world's champion ponies were given to Shirley. Here she takes her first drive behind Little Carnation, champion five-gaited pony presented by the Carnation Stables. She also owned Roan King II, a champion trick pony, given to her by Betsy King Ross, world's

champion girl trick rider, when the pony reached his age of retirement. Spunky, her first pony, was also a thoroughbred, whose real
name was Samuel of Speen. The Temples built a riding ring for
Shirley on the grounds of their present home in Brentwood.

Shirley hits the pool, finds it colder than she had anticipated.

CHAPTER 7

On the Set

Posing for still pictures is not nearly so much fun as making the actual moving picture. The publicity stills you see of movie scenes aren't clippings from the film. They're taken separately. The actors hold their poses after a scene is finished, and the director calls, "Okay for stills," and then the still cameraman goes to work.

When I was starting out in pictures, stills took longer than they do now, because cameras were not so far advanced. Color pictures took a whole second. That's longer than you would imagine, when you have to hold perfectly still. I used to pose for about 30 stills every day, and it was difficult to hold my pose, then hold it again for more shots, and then take another pose and do it all over again.

It grew pretty tiresome posing for fashion shots of the Shirley Temple dresses. Each dress would be photographed four times and since there were some 25 dresses, that made 100 shots, sometimes more, in one afternoon. Mom wouldn't let a dress be advertised with the Shirley Temple name unless I'd tried it on and we all liked it.

Posing for stills would have been even duller if Anthony Ugrin hadn't been my cameraman. Anthony was a grand person and we loved each other dearly, but he took an awful beating. Before he started working with me, everybody at Fox called him Tony when they wanted to annoy him, because that was a nickname he couldn't stand. When I first went to Fox, my pronunciation of "Anthony" sounded like "Anfunny." I had good strong lungs even at that early age, and after I'd yelled "Anfunny" across the set a few times, everybody at Fox from the directors to the property men was calling the poor man "Anfunny." It certainly sounded odd when a serious-minded director would yell, "Cut! Okay for stills, Anfunny!"

But that wasn't the worst thing that happened to Mr. Ugrin. Just about the time I got so I could say Anthony with a good honest "th," I discovered, to my glee, that the poor fellow had a distaste for being called Tony, so without any delay that's what I started calling him, and everybody on the set went back to Tony again. If you wanted him to do you a favor, though, you had to say Anthony.

Anthony, or Tony, or "Anfunny," did as good a job as anybody could have done to make posing for stills more interesting for me, so I'd have a natural expression. Sometimes he'd stand a pal of mine near the camera to make faces and cut up generally to make me laugh. People don't realize how much of a psychologist a really first-class photographer has to be. When you're playing a scene it's easy to be natural, because the story carries you along, but it's mighty hard to seem spontaneous in front of a still camera, and it's up to the photographer to make you relax.

I used all sorts of tricks to tease Anthony and keep him from getting pictures of me, when I felt mischievous. I'd screw up my face, or put up my arm to hide it, or take silly attitudes. He'd outfox me and take the picture anyhow, and then he'd show me the prints and kid me about how silly I looked, so then for a while I'd behave.

Sometimes Anthony would be asked to take pictures which probably bored him as much as they did me. They made me stick my head through calendars and grin like mad for New Year's pictures, and once they even posed me on schoolhouse steps with a lamb following me, for a Mary-Had-a-Little-Lamb picture.

Seasonal stills always had to be done ahead of time. About August I'd be posing, in all that California sunshine, for Christmas pictures. I'd hang up my stocking, and I'd wait up for Santa and fall asleep, and I'd discover my gifts on Christmas morning with wide-eyed glee, and all the time it would be four months before Christmas. In December, they'd dress me as a choirboy for Easter pictures, and in midsummer I'd pose with Thanksgiving turkeys. It was the same way with fashion shots. I'd pose for winter suits and velvet dresses in summer, and for playsuits and cottons in midwinter.

It's interesting to see how different photographers work. Some men make only a few pictures at one sitting, and go to great pains to get just the right pose, so everything will turn out perfect. Some prefer a simple character study and others use unusual backgrounds and props to make every picture tell a story. One Hollywood photographer always uses a plain white background and shoots very fast. You don't change position at all, just raise your eyes a bit or turn your head a fraction of an inch. He makes about 250 negatives at a sitting and throws three quarters of them away.

Anthony Ugrin told me a lot about how to act in front of a camera. For instance, he explained that when a profile shot was being made of me, posed with somebody else, I should turn my face three quarters of the way toward the camera and then look at the other person with just my eyes instead of my whole face. People used to call me a scene-stealer, when I was little (though I was totally unaware of it), and I think it was because of many camera tricks Anthony and others taught me when I was very young.

Costumes make a lot of difference in the way you feel while you're acting. In a costume like the green-and-silver brocade I wore for the dream scene in *The Little Princess,* you feel ladylike and graceful, and a minuet seems just the right kind of dance. In a sailor costume, like the pants and shirt for the hornpipe in *Captain January,* you feel tomboyish. And a raggedy costume, like the one I had in *Susannah of the Mounties,* makes you feel pathetic and poor.

It's a good thing I enjoyed costumes, because I always had a lot of fittings. But I loved to go over to the Women's Wardrobe at Fox. First Mom and I would look at sketches for new costumes. Then I'd go into the Blue Room, which was all mirrors and lush carpets, for my fittings. I had so many curls that it was hard for them to get my dresses on without mussing my hair, so Ande, our wardrobe woman, used to rip the shoulders of my dresses, and then sew them up afterwards so nicely that you couldn't tell they'd been opened.

Then I'd pay a visit to the workroom, which was even more

fascinating. Girls did their sewing at long tables, and there were marvelous dresses spilling all over everything, oceans of glamorous materials, like tulle, sewed with silver sequins, and yards of blue taffeta ruffles, and mountains of pink feathers, and drawers full of ribbons, and bows and spangles. The girls always liked to see how I looked in the costumes they had made for me, so when a dress was finished I would put it on and go in their big room and stand up on a table so they could see how beautiful the dress looked.

And then the shoemaker would come in to measure my foot for shoes, and I still remember how it tickled. The man who made my period shoes was a Frenchman, and we'd talk French together, so he had to worry about correcting my accent at the same time he was worrying about my soles and uppers.

There were padded figures of the Fox stars standing around in the workroom, with their names written on them, to save time on fittings. The Shirley Temple dummy looked very little and flat-chested beside them.

Every actress had a glass case filled with her dresses, and Ande would take me around and show them to me. I used to admire the most sirenish numbers that belonged to glamour stars like Alice Faye. There was one black satin gown with a very narrow skirt, slit to the knee, with black feathers all around the low neck, that I was fairly delirious about. Mom and I had quite a talk about how old I had to be before I could wear a dress like that. She said 20 and I said 16, so we compromised on 19.

Sadly enough, now that I'm almost old enough to wear a dress like that, it doesn't look so good to me any more. I don't suppose any woman ever gets to have a dress quite as glamorous as the one she dreams of having when she's a little girl.

After making a picture, Mom and I always took my costumes home to add to our collection. We have practically every dress I ever used in a picture. During the making of a picture, I would pick out the costume I liked best, and Ande would dress a doll in a miniature duplicate of that costume, made from scraps of the same material. Ande taught me to sew, too, and strange as it seems, I'm still capable of running up a blouse or playsuit for myself, though I don't get much time for it except on summer vacations.

156

As for make-up, I didn't wear any, even in *The Little Princess*, which was in Technicolor. There'd always be a make-up man on the set, though, and he'd always check my face just before they would start to shoot a scene. If you were too warm and your face became flushed, he would powder it lightly. Once there was a new make-up man on a picture I was making, and he kept holding up the scenes while he wiped and wiped away at my face. Finally I asked him if I should go and wash, and he said no, there was just one little spot that seemed noticeable. It turned out he was trying to brush away my dimple. You see, when I am serious the dimple turns into a tiny little bump. I told him please to leave it on, because whether it looked good to him or not, I was born with it.

In *The Littlest Rebel*, I had to wear blackface make-up. Sometimes that was fun, but sometimes it was exasperating and always messy. After going through four days with black make-up on, the director said we were finished and I was so happy. We went to my bungalow and Mom scrubbed my face, neck and hands until I was all pink and white again. We had no more than finished when the telephone rang and the director said that something had gone wrong with the camera and the scene had to be retaken; so I had to make up in blackface again and go back on the set.

The reason I wore black make-up was that I was supposed to be a little Southern girl, and as the Yankee soldiers were passing our house I pretended to be a pickaninny so I'd be safer. This was when I was only about 6, and because the make-believe in my pictures was so real to me and I was so tired of the black make-up I got mad and stamped my foot and asked if the Yanks couldn't take a different direction this time, and not go by my house, so I wouldn't have to get made up all over again.

I really got quite a cosmopolitan education out of the pictures I made at Fox. *Stowaway* was laid in China, *Wee Willie Winkie* in India, *Heidi* in Switzerland, and *The Little Princess* in England. The costumes and properties and sets were always pretty accurate, so you see I got a good idea of what all those countries were like.

After *Stowaway*, I almost felt as if I'd really been to China. There were about 50 Chinese children on the set for that picture, and they were swell. They were cute, and so polite about their Chinese-accented English sounds.

With my American friends I was very uppity about my 400 words of Chinese. I'd talk Chinese to them, and they'd say, "What's that mean, Shirley?" and I'd act surprised at their dumbness and answer, "Why, it means just what I said!"

My instructor was a young Chinese lady who taught Chinese at the University of California. She was being educated in American teaching methods so she could go back and help the Chinese government in Chiang Kai-shek's campaign to have everybody learn Mandarin. It seems that there are so many different Chinese dialects that people from one district can't understand people from another, and the government decided it would be best for everybody to learn one dialect, so they picked Mandarin instead of Cantonese because it's easier. The Chinese government was very appreciative when we used Mandarin in *Stowaway,* and they sent me a nice letter of thanks.

I met a number of Japanese people on the set, too. The whole crew of a Japanese destroyer came to see me, and once Kurusu, the snake in the grass who was Japan's ambassador to Washington when Pearl Harbor was bombed, came to visit me at Fox on his way to France. He grinned happily and was terribly polite.

He and his daughter had their pictures taken with me, and after Pearl Harbor an Australian magazine found that same picture in their files and used it. I thought that was kind of mean. Now, of course, I understand why Kurusu made such a big show of being friendly to me. He was pretending to be a pal so that nobody would suspect Japan's intentions, and he thought that Americans who enjoyed my movies would be pleased with the attention he paid me.

Turning to a more pleasant side of my cosmopolitan education, somebody I did enjoy meeting was Ginette Marboeuf-Hoyt, who won a contest as the little French girl who looked most like me. The contest was put on by one of the Fox agents in Paris, probably as a promotion stunt for my pictures. Three thousand five hundred mothers entered their daughters, and I guess that out of the 3,499 losers, 3,498 complained that their daughters looked more like me than Ginette did, so that was the last Shirley Temple contest held in France.

Martin Goodrider, who played with me in *Susannah of the Mounties,* was a real Blackfoot Indian, and I got a huge bang out of him. The studio sent to Montana for 12 Indian chiefs from Martin's tribe to work in the picture, and they lived in wigwams on the Fox lot for three weeks. They were most picturesque. How any work was done while the Indians were there, I don't know. We spent all of our time watching them. One of them looked as if he were the chief who posed for the Blackfoot Indian head on the buffalo nickel. Jiminy, he was impressive! They made me an honorary member of their tribe—an honorary Indian princess, with a name and costume.

They used to tease me a lot at Fox over being a good influence, because so many men on the staff suddenly started raising families while I was there. Doc Bishop became a father while he was doing publicity work for my pictures, and he swore that if it was a girl he'd name it Shirley Temple Bishop. Whether he was kidding or not, I got pretty excited while the baby was on its way, and every morning, first thing, I'd call up Doc and ask if he knew yet whether he had a son or a daughter. I was completely crushed when it turned out to be a boy.

I was a good influence in my pictures, too, because nearly always I was supposed to bring a couple of lovers together. Sometimes it was a married couple who couldn't get along until I fixed things, and sometimes it was a pair of sweethearts who quarrelled, and sometimes it was a lonely fellow who needed a wife, and Miss Shirley Fixit always found one for him. Maybe this had an effect on me, or maybe I'm just a natural matchmaker. Anyhow, I was always trying to promote romances for my friends.

Once, at least, I was successful, or so Ande tells me. Ande is quite a pretty woman. She must have been in her early thirties when I first met her, but for some reason she'd never been married. I just could not bear the idea of Ande's not being married, and I nagged and nagged at her about it, until finally she said, "All right, Shirley, I'll bring my fiancé to meet you."

Sure enough, she turned up with one of the tallest and handsomest fiancés a girl could want. It seems they'd been going together for years, but Ande hadn't quite been able to make up her mind to take the big step. But my teasing had actually helped her decide—unless, of course, she was just flattering me. We had a tremendous engagement shower for Ande in my dressing-room trailer.

I telephoned her at the wardrobe and asked her to come over for an afternoon coke with Klammie and me. Meanwhile, everybody on the set had piled up loads of packages in the trailer. Ande came in and everybody came up to the door of the trailer and screamed, "Surprise!" She certainly was surprised when she realized the packages were for her, and so pleased and excited that she cried. There were a number of lovely satin slips and nightgowns, and Mom and I gave her a blue velvet dressing gown. That was a high point in my life.

Then there was the romance Anthony and I created for Klammie, who wasn't married either, but this romance was strictly a gag. There was a make-up man on the set who was eccentric, but definitely. He was a wild-eyed vegetarian who ate nothing except raisins and nuts, and sometimes he'd treat himself to a raw carrot.

He was the one Anthony and I picked as a romantic suitor for Klammie. The idea really was funny, because though Klammie had plenty of fun in her, she was very sedate and ladylike. The gag must have bored her dreadfully, especially since Anthony and I kept insisting for months that she and this man were secretly in love. But she was a good sport. The great ambition of our lives was to get them together for a snapshot, but since they worked on opposite sides of the studio and didn't even know each other to speak to, this was difficult, and we never managed it.

For Valentine's Day and Christmas, Shirley made colorful paper gifts for her friends at Fox.

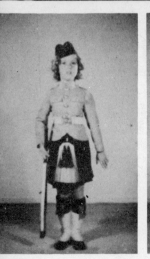

Wee Willie Winkie pleased Shirley because of a foreign set and costumes. Khyber Pass scenes were filmed near Hollywood, in a location whose topography is said to resemble closely the famous Indian

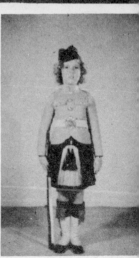

pass. Hollywood's conversion of Kipling's drummer boy into a girl proved rewarding, for *Wee Willie Winkie's* gross world receipts met the average for a Temple picture—$10,000,000.

A group of Boy Scouts who had won their Eagles came to the Fox studio, where Shirley pinned on the Eagle badges, played the piano while they sang Scout songs, then entertained them at lunch.

Honorary National Sponsor of Airmail Week was the title conferred upon Shirley by Postmaster General James Farley. She drew this poster, sent all over the country to publicize airmail service.

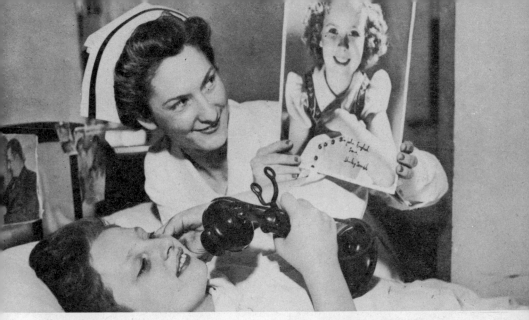

This 14-year-old boy, dying in a Chicago hospital, had a "crush" on Shirley. She sent him an autographed picture, telephoned long distance to cheer him up.

When Fox decided she was growing up, Shirley abandoned the multitudinous curls for this hairdress which she first wore in *Rebecca of Sunnybrook Farm*. She congratulates Walt Disney on his "Oscar."

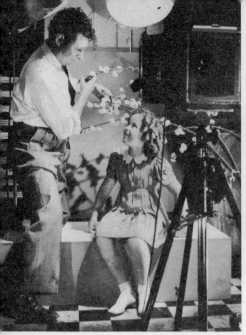

Left, Shirley is glamourized by George Hurrell, ace Hollywood photographer. Right, Vincent Astor fixes her camera.

Shirley's fervor for collecting autographs equalled that of the autograph hounds who sought hers. Even Al Smith signed her album.

Suave Gertrude Lawrence played horse for Shirley in Bermuda and gave a tea party in Shirley's honor.

With Darryl Zanuck, Fox's vice-president in charge of production, at a preview of *The Little Princess*.

In her private playground at home Shirley takes a hurdle on the miniature chute-the-chute.

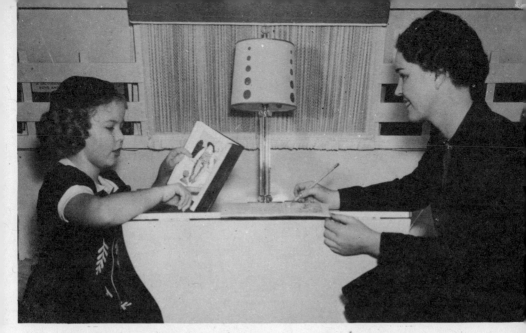

With Klammie in the bungalow. Miss Klampt is still at Fox, teaches a school consisting of half a dozen child players.

Shirley sucks a Hawaiian lollipop. At the other end of the sugar cane is one of the friends she made on her trip to Hawaii.

Shirley bought a $10 camera in Bermuda, took it along on her third Hawaiian trip. The pictures which follow are authentic specimens of photographs made by her when she returned to the studio.

Before a movie scene is shot, a placard identifying it is held up before the camera. Here is Paul Lockwood, assistant cameraman on *The Little Princess*.

George Temple photographed by Shirley. She was able to take indoor pictures with her inexpensive equipment because the brilliant

Mary Lou Isleib takes Shirley's place as a cameraman gauges the intensity of the light which falls upon her hair. Even hair as blonde as Mary Lou's and Shirley's can photograph dark.

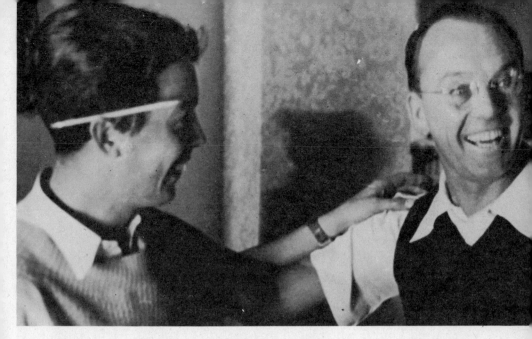

Technicolor lighting made the Fox set as bright as day. A propman and assistant director pose genially for Shirley's camera.

Anthony Ugrin, Shirley's still cameraman during her entire career at Fox, peers from behind a drapery to get an unposed picture of Shirley, finds himself photographed by her instead.

Left, Anita Louise, who played in *The Little Princess*. Right, fans peering through the Temple gates to catch a glimpse of Shirley.

Left, Mary Nash, actress, and Klammie. Right, Arthur Treacher, of whom Shirley writes in an earlier chapter, "He is the only person in the world who can neigh with an English accent."

174

Left, Buck, the dog star, with a 6-week-old deer. Right, the parrot which was part of the cast of *The Little Princess*.

Left, two of Shirley's dog pets are rounded up in the kennel for feeding. Right, her pony, Spunky, at home in California after his cross-country trip.

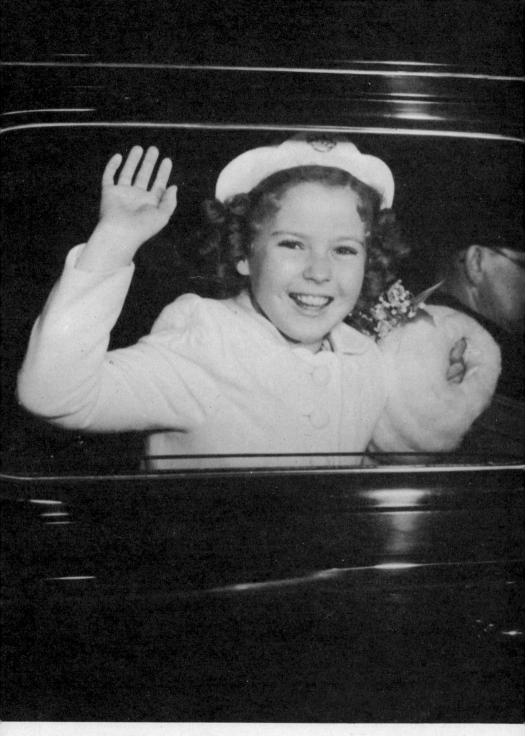

Shirley enjoyed a première as much as the thousands of fans who thronged to see her in person.

CHAPTER 8

"Dear Shirley"

Letters are a big thing in your life when you're in pictures. Not only do people write you if they think you're good, but they also write and tell you if there's any little thing they don't like.

The studio always kept an ear cocked to what people said in my fan mail. Sometimes even before a picture was released, they'd get so many letters from people who had read articles about the picture that they'd make changes. For instance, *Dimples* was originally called *The Bowery Princess,* but there were so many objections to my being associated with the Bowery that they changed the title.

Fox never let me be spanked in a picture. Director John Ford once planned such a scene, but the studio would not okay it.

In *Captain January,* I did a hula dance, with a little grass skirt and a flower lei, and when the advance pictures came out, so many people objected that they took out the hula scene and used a hornpipe called the "Codfish Ball."

Fox was kind of worried, too, about the scene in *Susannah of the Mounties* where I smoked a pipe. The way they played it first, I didn't get sick, but the Indian boy I was smoking with got "sick as a dog." Then they decided that if I smoked without getting sick it would set a bad example to the country's children, so in order to discourage young people from the filthy weed, they had me get

177

sick after all.

Guess it's a good thing that the children who went to my pictures couldn't see me in my off moments, when I was naughty, because I was supposed to be a model child. One group of fans organized the International Shirley Temple Club, or the Templers. The rules were Obey Promptly, Be Clean and Neat, Study Faithfully, and Be Kind and Thoughtful. I was supposed to do all those things, and I bet some of those kids just hated me.

Mom and I used to get lovely letters from people who enjoyed my pictures. Every once in a while, someone would write in wanting to adopt me, if they'd seen a picture in which I was supposed to be an orphan. There were loads of invitations to be flower girl at weddings of people I didn't even know. It would have been fun to accept every one of them, because I adore weddings.

Then there were requests for ringlets of my hair to make bracelets. They weren't all sentimental requests, either, because one man wrote that he could make plenty of money selling them if we'd only co-operate and send him enormous amounts of my curly locks. If all the requests for my hair had been fulfilled, in a very short time I would have been absolutely bald.

Some of the letters that came in were very funny. One little girl from Detroit wrote that her parents had taken her to see *Little Miss Marker,* and they laughed like anything when I said, "Ah nuts!" so she said it too next day at Sunday dinner, and she was sent away from the table. She wanted to know how I got away with it. At that time I wasn't able to write, but Mom and I decided to tell her that some things are funnier on the screen than in real life.

Another gem was a letter from a 10-year-old boy who wrote, "Although you are only 5 and probably cannot read, perhaps you will send me your photograph with your signature on it, if you can write, which I doubt."

I used to get many oversized letters and telegrams. When they held Children's Week at Atlantic City, I received a telegram 10 feet high asking me to come. Another time the largest postcard ever sent through the mails came to me, an Easter greeting signed by 5,000 little girls of Hutchinson, Kansas. It was 8 feet by 4, strictly prewar stuff. Imagine trying to get away with it today, with the postal department overworked like it is!

Until he died about a year ago, one of the blind veterans at the Veterans' Home in Sawtelle, California, used to write me regularly. It was a little difficult to read his letters because he sometimes struck the wrong typewriter keys, but I always answered them.

One girl wrote and scolded me for sending a picture of myself to her boy friend. He'd asked for the picture, and he'd gotten it, just like anyone else, but she seemed to think it was personal.

Two boys who evidently weren't making as good an impression as they might with their girls wrote and asked me for personally autographed photographs, to make the girls jealous.

Some of the most interesting mail comes from servicemen. They're such nice, decent kids. They don't seem to think that they're doing anything more in the war than just what they ought to do, and they're so brave and modest. When they write in and ask for a picture, I feel honored and humble to think that men who are risking their lives every day for my safety get pleasure out of having a picture of me in their barracks.

One boy wrote me from the South Pacific and in the middle of the letter he said, "Time out for an air raid." Then he went on and added, "Back again, nobody hurt, thank heavens!" Then there was a whole pack of letters from a group of Marines who were writing on behalf of a buddy. They said he was in love with me and asked me to send him a picture. "He'd be a pretty good Marine if he could get you off his mind," they said. We used to call this kind of letter the "John Alden" type, because the boy never wrote any himself. Of course I think it might have been a gag his buddies dreamed up to tease him.

The most tragic letter came from a boy who had lost a leg in battle. He sent me a picture of himself in his Marine dress uniform and wanted to know whether I could tell which was his real leg and which was the artificial one. And he also asked me whether it would make any difference if I had a sweetheart who came back from the wars with one leg gone. Well, it really was impossible to tell which was the real leg, and I wrote him so, and I also wrote him that any girl who loved a man wouldn't care a bit if he had lost a leg in the war, but would be proud of him and love him all the more. Probably he was afraid to ask his real sweetheart about it, and asked me because he thought I was a typical American girl. I certainly hope his sweetheart feels the same way. She's not much of a woman if she doesn't.

There was one letter that made me feel creepy. It came from a boy with the American forces in Germany. He found one of my childhood pictures on the wall of a house which the Germans had used as headquarters before the Allies took the town. Right above it was a picture of Hitler. The boy sent my picture back to me with a note saying, "I didn't think you'd like the company you were in, Shirley, so I'm returning your picture."

Another of my baby pictures was found by an American soldier in the pocket of a dead Japanese sniper. I just don't understand the Japanese, and I don't suppose anyone else does, either. The soldier who killed the Japanese wrote, "Sorry to treat a fan of yours so badly, Shirley," and sent me my picture as a souvenir. Jiminy, I felt funny.

Some few of the letters are truly terrific. One boy in Portugal writes me regularly, all about the fatal beauty of my eyes and stuff. He says he's in love with me and wants to marry me, but he wants me to realize clearly that in Portugal there's no divorce! P.S. I declined, and not because I believe in divorces; I definitely do not!

The Chinese write more graceful letters than any other people. If they ask for a picture, and send money, they usually write that the money is not enclosed to pay for the picture, because it is priceless, but is rather to cover the expense of sending it.

There's something very heart-warming about knowing that people all over the world, people I haven't even seen, have enjoyed my films so much that they feel a personal friendship for me and want my pictures. Some of them send me wonderful presents, too, even if they haven't met me, as a kind of thank-you gift for movies that gave them pleasure. "Dear Shirley," they write, "I hope you like this."

One couple we met has been sending me gorgeous table silver over a period of years, and now I've got practically a complete set—which may come in handy in a couple of years, when Jack and I take the big step!

A man who is a member of a big manufacturing firm has sent

me a really beautiful present on my birthday, April 23, for the past 10 years. Halfway around the year to my next birthday, he sends me a slightly less elaborate present, and on the 23rd of every month, he sends flowers. I've never even seen him.

Fans all around the world helped me build up my doll collection, which numbered 1,561 when last counted. They almost moved us out of the house, so we had to build a special room for them. The collection was just a happenstance. It began way back when I made *Bright Eyes*. I fell in love with the doll in the picture (I called it Pinkie), so Winfield Sheehan gave it to me. After that, quite a few people at the studio began giving me dolls, and the Fox publicity department began talking about "Shirley Temple's doll collection."

Well, then the fans really became generous. Not only individuals but delegations and clubs and dollmakers and foreign countries sent dolls to me. Fox arranged to have the distributors of their films in every country send me dolls dressed in the national costumes, so my knowledge of dress in foreign countries grew. There is a group of American Indian and Alaskan dolls, made of everything from dried apples to cornhusks, which represent a score of tribes. Our housekeeper, Katie, gave me three beautiful German dolls dressed in national costume, from some of her relatives. There are two Irish character dolls, "Shanneen Tom," the storyteller, and an old crone named "Old Breeze" who is a professional "keener"—that means a weeper at funerals. There are dolls from every province in France and Italy, and a Russian doll that is really a disguised tea cozy, and a miniature African warrior in full regalia, which Osa Johnson sent me. John McCormack sent a wonderful tiny green Irish leprechaun, and Bill Robinson gave me two carved replicas of himself. One whistles "Yankee Doodle" and the other "Susy Q."

There are many dolls from Lenci, the Italian dollmaker. Then there are doll replicas of Princess Elizabeth of England and the Dionne quintuplets, and replicas of Gainsborough's "Blue Boy" and Reynolds' "Age of Innocence" and Thomas Lawrence's "Pinky." There's the Old Woman Who Lived in a Shoe, with all her children, about three quarters of an inch long. There's my own pet favorite, Raggedy Ann, that I played with for years, who's been

181

washed about a million times. And there's a native doll picked up by my dentist during the New Guinea campaign!

But dolls weren't the only things given to me by my fan friends. They gave me everything, including animals. I do believe that fans have sent me practically every kind of animal except a giraffe and a hippopotamus. One fan club sent me a cow, after they saw *Rebecca*. The cow didn't stand its trip very well, though, and we sent it to a farm to recuperate.

One of the most dramatic episodes of my career at Fox came when some Australian fans sent me a present of two wallabies. They arrived at the studio, and the minute we were through work, I wanted to look at them, so we went over to see them with Charlie Goldie, one of the Fox people, and a Fox representative from Australia who happened to be visiting the studio at that time.

They were very cute, like tiny kangaroos, with long, long tails. I wanted to take them out of the crate and play with them. The Australian man said he could handle them okay, so he took them out of the crate and tied them to a tree.

One of them slipped the rope and off he bounded like a streak of lightning. Until you have seen a wallaby in full flight, you have never seen anything. They use the tail for a kind of lever, to push and steer by, and they go bounce, bounce, bounce, so fast it's hardly believable.

Well, the wallaby took flight. Charlie Goldie and the Australian got a head start, but in no time at all everyone in that vicinity joined the chase, and there were executives and publicity people and secretaries and actors and directors and grips and propmen all dashing after the wallaby, to see the fun, with me bringing up the rear laughing so I could hardly run. It was just like a chase scene in a corny comedy.

The wallaby seemed to want green grass and trees, so he headed for the permanent gardens, which are very formal, with flower beds and a pool, and he bounced around there for a while. The men kept yelling at each other to try to corner him, but the wallaby outsmarted them every time. Finally he took one great leap and jumped head first into the pool. The poor little wallaby didn't know there wasn't any water in the pool, and there he lay, knocked out cold. That was the end of the wild chase. One of the men jumped in the dry pool and picked him up and carried him back to his crate.

I was terribly worried and wanted to get a doctor for the wallaby, but in a very few minutes the little fellow started to come to. Apparently wallabies are tough. I did my best to persuade Mom to let me take the wallabies home and keep them with my other animals, but of course after that experience I didn't have a chance, so we gave the wallabies to the zoo and there I visited them regularly.

Fan mail is an excellent mirror by which to gauge yourself. The criticisms are usually well-founded and it's gratifying to know people care enough about you and your career to make constructive suggestions. Another reassuring thing about the people who write me—they aren't fickle. They've always believed in me. Even when I made *The Bluebird* for Fox, which I learned in later years was not too successful, they stood by me and fan mail poured in at the same rate for the year and four months of my temporary retirement. As a youngster, the worry and responsibility as to whether a picture was good or a great financial success did not bother me in the least. My chief interest was my great joy in making it. I always worked very sincerely and very hard and loved every minute of it. Leading the box-office poll meant very little to me. I knew it was an honor and that was all as far as I was concerned.

Nobody knows why a picture flops. Some people thought *The Bluebird* was made so soon after *Wizard of Oz* that audiences weren't in the mood for another fantasy. Some thought it was too imaginative anyhow. Others thought it didn't have enough story, but was merely a succession of pretty scenes which gave the cast no chance to act. It was funny but Mom and Daddy hadn't wanted me to make *The Bluebird* and even asked our attorney, Lloyd Wright, to protest the part, which he did in a very nice letter to the heads of the studio. Mom and Daddy felt too few people would really understand this fairy tale which was written originally for highly adult audiences. But the studio officials thought otherwise.

The Fox people were upset, because they'd been living in dread of my growing up. They had even taken a year off my age, in all publicity releases. That was something I never knew about until

I thought I was having my twelfth birthday, and Mom told me it was really my thirteenth. I cried because I felt I'd lost a year of my life, but when the tears dried I began to feel proud of being so mature. The point, of course, was that Fox knew that very few youthful stars, with some brilliant exceptions like Mary Pickford, go on to success in grown-up roles. The studio executives were scared stiff that poor old Temple would be a box-office has-been at the age of twelve.

On my side, though I loved the people at Fox very much indeed, I was beginning to realize my story material wasn't holding up too well. My pictures were usually the type known as "vehicles"—that is, they were built around my personality. And that personality was always the same—so darned sweet and angelic that I never had to do any real acting or branch out and learn to take other kinds of parts. Once, just once, how I would have loved to be really disagreeable on the screen!

EXECUTIVE DEPARTMENT
Office of the Mayor
ATLANTIC CITY, N. J.

APRIL 4, 1938.

MISS SHIRLEY TEMPLE,
HOLLYWOOD, CALIF.
DEAR SHIRLEY –

ON BEHALF OF ALL OF OUR CITIZENS I AM
EXTENDING A MOST SINCERE INVITATION TO YOU
TO COME TO ATLANTIC CITY, AS OUR GUEST, FOR
CHILDREN'S WEEK, JUNE 24 TO JULY 1.

THE AFFAIR IS AN ANNUAL EVENT DURING
WHICH THE RESORT PROVIDES A SPECIAL PROGRAM
FOR ITS YOUNGER GUESTS FROM ALL SECTIONS OF
THE WORLD. EVERY DAY OFFERS SOMETHING NEW
IN THE WAY OF ENTERTAINMENT AND WE ARE SURE
YOU WOULD HAVE A MOST ENJOYABLE VISIT.

WE HAVE BEEN GIVEN TO UNDERSTAND THAT
YOU WILL BE IN THE EAST AT THAT TIME AND WE
HOPE THAT YOU WILL FIND IT POSSIBLE TO ACCEPT
THIS INVITATION TO COME TO ATLANTIC CITY.

SINCERELY,

C. D. White

MAYOR

ATLANTIC CITY

This giant invitation would have overwhelmed anyone less accustomed to public adulation than Shirley.

These photographs of Shirley at different ages were sent out in answer to fan requests. Most of them were actually signed by Shirley.

Current requests for pictures of Shirley keep two full-time secretaries and one part-time secretary at work in the Temple home.

Last Christmas Shirley received Christmas cards from American servicemen everywhere in the world, as well as hundreds of cards from foreign soldiers, particularly the Chinese, with whom she is especially popular. The "Fox Division" of a warship sent her five dozen pink roses, and scores of other gifts arrived from unknown admirers.

188

Future Dreams To Come True

1936 picture I am on "The Littlest Rebel"

By Bill Weir

Self Portrait

Sometimes an admirer will add a postscript saying, "Dear Secretary, please give me a break and show this to Shirley." Servicemen often write to tell Shirley they have bet a month's pay on receiving a personally autographed picture. One soldier sent in the sketches of Shirley and himself (above). Shirley does her best to answer all requests from servicemen.

189

Dwarfed by the klieg lights, heavy costume and massive set, Shirley sits on her throne, disinterested in the "juicers," script girls, wardrobe men, directors, make-up crew and cameramen, ready to shoot the dream scene from *The Little Princess*.

When moviegoers saw the finished scene they had no way of reckoning the painstaking time and effort which went into shooting a perfect "take." Make-up is invariably considered necessary for Technicolor, but when Shirley took three screen tests, one with the regular make-up, one with powder only, and one with no make-up at all, the third proved best. Since California law forbade Shirley to work at night, Fox had to stretch black canvas over two stage blocks to create an artificial night for the scene when Shirley goes to the hospital to seek her father. This film, laid in England around 1890, was called by Darryl Zanuck, "the finest motion picture with which I have ever been associated." It was the last of the truly great successes which Shirley scored for Twentieth Century-Fox.

191

THE LITTLE PRINCESS

Shirley plays the part of "Sara," a little girl whose father goes off to the Boer War, leaves her in a boarding school in the "care" of a heartless headmistress. Orphaned and dispossessed by his reported death, she is mistreated, escapes, finds her father in a veterans' hospital. A minor plot thread concerns the love of a teacher and riding master, played by Anita Louise and Richard Greene.

1. Shirley and Arthur Treacher, who was "Bubbling Bertie," out-mug one another offstage.

4. "Bertie" shows her the latest dances, picked up during his career in the music halls.

5. "Miss Michin" gives "Sara" a party, interrupted by "Captain Crewe's" reported death.

2. "Sara" promises her father, "Captain Crewe," to be a "good soldier" when he leaves.

3. "Miss Rose," one of the teachers, comforts "Sara" when homesickness sets in.

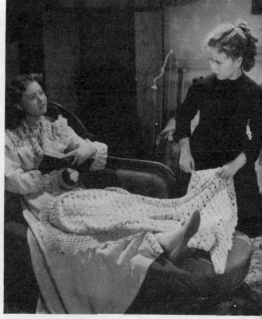

6. When "Miss Michin" learns he died bankrupt, she sends the ex-heiress to an attic room.

7. The other girls change their attitude, treat "Sara" as a servant and abuse her.

8. "Becky," the scullery maid, is her only friend. They are about to run away when . . .

9. . . ."Ran Dass," a Hindu servant next door, surprises them with clothes, food and gifts.

12. When she sees "Miss Michin" and the police enter the hospital she runs for cover, hides behind a soldier's wheelchair. As they are about to apprehend her she sees the soldier is her father.

10. Believing her father is still alive, "Sara" slips away and sets out to find him.

11. She strays into a veterans' hospital where "Queen Victoria" is visiting the wounded.

13. He recognizes her immediately. "Bertie," "Sara" and "Captain Crewe" are reunited. They stand at rigid attention as "Queen Victoria" leaves and the film ends.

A typical crowd of Temple fans waiting to see *The Little Princess*.
Note the number of men. Shirley's appeal was not confined to children and mothers, and her fan mail came from every type of person.

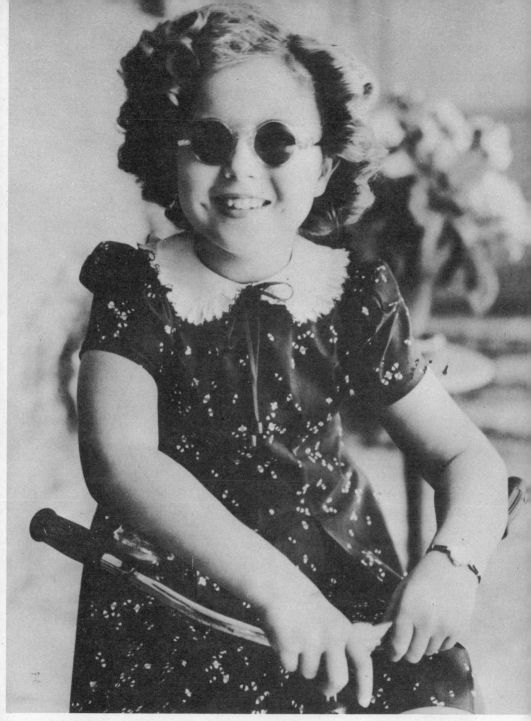

No star has ever received the amount of public attention given to Shirley. Like Garbo, whom she consistently outdrew as a box-office attraction, Shirley protects herself with dark glasses.

197

Attached as she was to the fabulous dolls, Shirley confides that her real pride and joy was a trunkful of guns she once collected.

This lace-timmed doll was sent to Shirley by an admirer in Paris.
It is one of the largest in her collection.

Even Shirley's earliest doll, a battered Raggedy Ann, is protected by professional glass cases. The miniature cottage is peopled by

dolls to scale. Although Shirley no longer plays with them, the Temples are reluctant to give the collection to a museum.

In *Susannah of the Mounties,* her twentieth feature picture, Shirley played an orphan from a waylaid wagon train. Fox spared no expense for authenticity, imported 12 Blackfoot Indians from the U.S. Indian Service, put up a $25,000 bond for their return.

But for *The Bluebird* the studio went even further. Designers' sketches for the sets indicate the lavish production planned for the film. *The Bluebird,* filmed in Technicolor with an outstanding cast, was among Fox's most expensive films.

In this scene from *The Bluebird*, Shirley and Johnny Russell, as
"Mityl" and "Tityl," leave their grandparents, played by Al
Sheehan and Cecelia Loftus, as they set out to seek the bluebird of
happiness. This artistically beautiful film was the first Temple
picture to fail at the box office, led to Fox's abrogation of Shirley's contract. Though it was withdrawn from most first-run houses

after a few days, Fox made good its expenditure on second-run and foreign trade. Shirley's partisans felt that the failure of the picture was due to the general unpopularity of fantasies and to the fact that it gave Shirley no chance to act. She could undoubtedly have found an immediate welcome in other studios, but her desire for a normal school life led the Temples to make other plans.

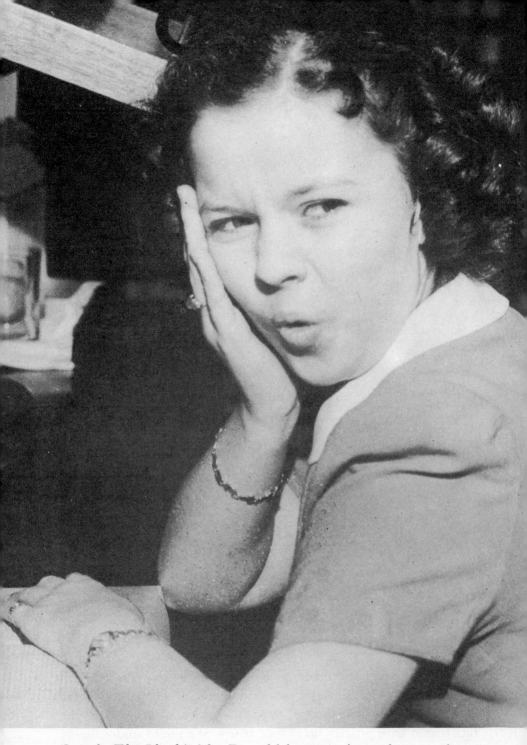

"I made *The Bluebird* for Fox which, to put it gently, was a box-office floperoo!"

206

CHAPTER 9

School Days

Although the poor showing of *The Bluebird,* plus the "problem" of my growing up, suggested the advisability of temporary retirement for me, there were more important reasons why the family decided to put me in school. Probably the biggest one was that Mom and Daddy were both beginning to wonder if I wasn't missing a lot by never having the school experience other girls have. Somehow, I just didn't want to grow up without knowing a whole crowd of girls, and studying with them, and being one of their gang, instead of having to make a whole new set of friends on every picture. So at the age of eleven, my little personal world changed completely. Picture-making stopped being the big thing in my life, and Westlake School for Girls took its place. I started in the seventh grade, and graduated in June, 1945.

For the next three years, I stayed away from the screen almost completely. After *The Bluebird,* I made only one more picture for Fox. It was *Young People,* with Jack Oakie. At least, after having made something like four pictures a year since I was 5, it seemed to me as if I were staying away. Actually, I made two pictures between leaving Fox and signing up with David Selznick. *Kathleen,* for Metro-Goldwyn-Mayer, was fun because it marked the first time I'd worn a long evening dress and had been glamorous for a camera. *Miss Annie Rooney,* for Edward Small, was fun because of

the jitterbug scenes, and because Dickie Moore was playing opposite me.

But my heart was at Westlake, not in movies, during all this
time. If that sounds sentimental, it's probably because I'm still
so close to graduation. At Westlake it wasn't traditional to cry
at graduation but we made up for it on Poets' Day. The girls read
poems and sang songs about the dear old school; how we'd all
learned to be fine noble women, with the result one wept buckets.
I always cried on Poets' Day with all the rest of them. As I look
back and think of the cotillions, and the outdoor barbecues on
spring evenings, and the wisteria by the tennis court, I miss it all
dreadfully.

When I started to Westlake, the autumn term already had begun,
so Mom had to make special arrangements with the principal to
admit me. It's a private school for girls, in Holmby Hills, near
enough to our home so that I could be driven there in a few minutes.
Since it's a boarding school as well as a day school, it seemed like
a second home even to the day students.

The first day Mom and I drove up we saw the beautiful white
building in the hills, with trees and lawns. Some girls my age were
playing games outside, and I wondered whether any of them
would turn out to be my good friends. Then we went into the
office, and Mom introduced me to Miss Mills. As I listened to some
music students practicing scales and arpeggios in another room
I wondered whether any of *them* would be my friends.

Mom was sad because she was going to leave me at Westlake for
the day, and go away while I learned to get along by myself. But
I felt wonderful. My first class was French, and it was already in
session. Miss Mills took me by the hand into the classroom and
introduced me to Madame, and went away. All the girls were sitting
at their desks stiff as ramrods, and when I came in they giggled.
I thought that was the way they always greeted a new girl, so I
took it with aplomb, as we say in French! Afterwards, I found out
they'd been wondering about me ever since they had heard I was
coming. They thought I'd probably be snooty, and they had decided to make sure that if anybody got snubbed, it wouldn't be
they.

Madame put me at a double desk with a cute, plump, red-haired girl. That girl was wonderful to me. She seemed to understand that I didn't want to be snooty to anyone and that I was just crazy to have the girls accept me as one of themselves, for my own sake, not because I was in the movies. She really mothered me. Incidentally, she now has one of the most gorgeous figures in the world and she was our May queen during senior year!

Because of their theory that I must be a conceited brat, a clique of the more sophisticated girls in my class decided to make me feel uncomfortable. They didn't talk to me, and they said things in my hearing like, "We'll have that party with just our own little group of friends." It didn't bother me too much, because I didn't know anything about how girls act at school, and I never realized how snooty they were being. So I ignored them right back, and they changed very quickly. By the end of the first two months I had become one of the gang.

I never received or wanted any special privileges. Even when I was working on a picture, my teachers didn't make allowances for me in my school work. Sometimes other girls and I went on field trips to museums and libraries, or had a luncheon party in a restaurant. On these outside trips, I disliked to be recognized, and actually, I seldom was. At school we wore uniforms just alike, flat-heeled shoes; no make-up or jewelry was allowed. You almost had to look twice to tell us apart. Sometimes people I knew very well came to Westlake and didn't recognize me.

Once a French scholar named Dr. Paul Perigord gave us a lecture to pep us up about what an easy and beautiful language French is. He started off with a story about Adolphe Menjou and Shirley Temple. According to the story, it seemed that Mr. Menjou telephoned Shirley to say hello and find out how she was, and she said, "Oh, I'm not so good. I'm having a tough time with my French." And Mr. Menjou said, "Well, I'll tell you how to learn 500 French words in one minute."

So Shirley was naturally thrilled at this prospect, because she didn't like memorizing vocabularies any better than anyone else does, so she said quickly, "How?" and Mr. Menjou explained, "Well, Shirley, you see, every word that ends in -*ion* is the same in French as it is in English."

By the time poor Dr. Perigord was through with his little story, every girl in the audience was laughing, and he couldn't understand why. Probably he thought something was wrong with his tie and collar, or that he'd made a mistake in English. But they were laughing because I was sitting right under his nose, in the front row, and he hadn't recognized me.

Another time Charles Laughton came to have tea with a small group of us at school, and to read us some passages from the Bible and Shakespeare. He was sitting in a big chair, and we were all sitting around him on the floor, and he kept looking at me. Finally, he said, "Don't I know you?"

We'd been together on a radio broadcast for China Relief, but he didn't recognize me, and I had a wonderful time teasing him. I said, innocently, "Well, I went to a radio broadcast where you were speaking."

He wasn't satisfied with that, and said, "No, I've met you somewhere. Do I know your father?"

Still innocent, I said, "Maybe you do. Who is my father?" None of the girls gave me away, though they were giggling like mad. Finally Miss Mills took pity on him and told him who I was.

After I'd been at Westlake a few months, the only girls who seemed conscious of my being in the movies were girls who didn't know me. My friends and classmates forgot all about it, and so did I, while I was at school.

When I went to a party, it was the same way. Even when I didn't know the children, they regarded me as one of the crowd when they saw that's what I wanted. Once a writer asked me if my reputation didn't frighten boys away, and I said no, but sometimes I wished it did. Of course, that was before I became engaged.

I started having my first real dates when I was a sophomore, but they didn't seem terribly thrilling to me, because I'd been going to school parties where boys had been invited. What does stand out in my mind is a hop I went to at West Point. There were 400 or 500 stags, and they cut in on me so fast that finally they all just lined up and had me go down the line and dance a few steps with each one. Jiminy, I felt glamorous. They were so particular about introducing me to every boy, though, that the introductions took more time than the dancing.

At Westlake all of us older girls, including myself, were constantly being asked for advice on How to Charm Men. My own theory was that a girl should forget about using a line and be herself. Some girls I know believe in acting bored. They think it shows sophistication. That's silly. But I don't agree with other girls who act too interested in a boy whether they like him or not, and pretend to hang on every word he utters, even when they are bored stiff. It's more fun and less exertion to find something that you're both sincerely interested in, and talk about it, instead of breaking your neck trying to act like a siren, which terrifies most boys.

Another thing the younger girls talked to me about was their family troubles. Quite a lot of them came from broken homes. There wasn't much you could say to cheer them up, but I did my best. Believe me, there's never going to be a Hollywood divorce for this child.

I enjoyed the Westlake cotillions more than any other dances. We had five cotillions a year, for the four upper classes. The Mother's Club sponsored them and different classes took turns acting as hostesses. We took a vote on whether they were to be formal or not. Almost always, we decided to go formal. Come April, every girl in the world wanted a new spring date dress, and if a party was coming up, we would make it a good excuse to get a dress out of the parents.

We did our own decorating for the dances at Halloween, Christmas or Valentine's Day. They were held in the Great Hall, a big beautiful ballroom with two staircases. I always envied girls who lived at school, because they could float down those stairs so effectively in their evening dresses, while I and the other girls who lived at home just had our dates call for us in the usual manner and came in wearing our wraps.

Air Cadets or boys in the V-12 training program came to the cotillions, and there was a date committee to get blind dates for girls who wanted them. Jiminy, how we worried over the dates! We figured out compatibility on a basis of age, height, weight, mutual interests, and even coloring. Sometimes the dates were a complete bust, and sometimes a Beautiful Thing developed. Generally I served on the blind-date committee, but since I wasn't a class officer I didn't have final say on whether or not Joe and Karen were both really to go with each other.

Pictures took up so much of my time that I couldn't be as active in school clubs as I would have liked. Mom did more than I did. She was a Mothers' Club officer. I sang in the Glee Club, and wrote a secret gossip column for the school paper, and I had small parts in the various school entertainments. Once I was offered a big part, but I didn't want to take it, partly because I was afraid people would think I was showing off, and partly because I knew I'd have to be just sensationally good before an audience of my friends and their mothers, and it frightened me. I had a part in the Vox Varieties last spring, which is a sort of super-vaudeville show we put on every spring to pay for the class annual, but I had to give it up when I went into *Kiss and Tell*. Because it was impossible to do both, all I did was coach some girls in a Hawaiian number.

It sounds as if I were as much interested in my social life at school as in my studies, and I'll admit freely that was true. I wasn't what you'd call a really eager student. When I entered Westlake, I had very little trouble with the school work, because my studio teachers had given me a good background. But the other girls fascinated me so that I kept looking at them instead of my books. My marks were not so good the first year, but they kept getting better as I went on, and in my last year I had a B average.

When I was tiny, I remember that my first teacher at Fox, even before Klammie, was Miss Lillian Barkley, who was a Phi Beta Kappa. Her key intrigued me so much that I announced I was going to be a Phi Beta Kappa some day, and after that they teased me by calling me the Phi Beta Kappa of the industry. But right now it doesn't look as if I'd ever make the grade, even if I should change my mind and go to college. I'm just too much interested in having fun with my friends, and making pictures.

We were seriously interested in politics and the war at Westlake, though. We read *Time* and *Newsweek* in classes, and that gave us the habit, and most of us kept up with current events in the summers, too. And at lunch time we sometimes got into very heated arguments on the war and the peace. Before the Roosevelt-Dewey election, we argued all the time, so don't think we discussed only clothes and boys, though we did cover those subjects, too!

Left, Shirley rides behind the camera on the *Young People* set. Right, Shirley has her first formal date and wears her first long evening gown. The gown was white, with dubonnet ribbons, dubonnet hairbow and silver slippers. The occasion was the commencement ball of California Military Academy. The escort was Cadet Captain Raymond Berlinger. This picture was taken during Shirley's temporary retirement.

Seated on the piano bench, in the foreground, Shirley sings with the other members of her Campfire Girls troop, whom she is entertaining in her home. Shirley had a sincere desire to be accepted by other girls on their own terms, succeeded in making friends

and classmates almost forget her stardom. On the wall is an oil portrait of Shirley at the age of 7, when she was the world's best-known child.

When Shirley was 12, Metro-Goldwyn-Mayer signed her at a salary of $2,500 a week to make *Kathleen*. Here M-G-M stars Mickey Rooney and Judy Garland show her around her new studio.

In *Kathleen,* movie-goers saw Shirley in evening dress for the first
time. The film told of a lonely girl's efforts to win the love of an
indifferent father. It was moderately successful.

At Westlake, Shirley wore simple school uniforms, was given no special privileges, was required to make up work missed while working on films. The Westlake principal believes that teachers, in an effort to avoid favoritism, were unusually strict with Shirley.

Shirley's first movie kiss was given her by Dickie Moore in *Miss Annie Rooney*, filmed by Edward Small, an independent producer. Matchmaker in all her earlier films, here a new grown-up Shirley carried the romantic lead.

This jitterbug sequence from *Miss Annie Rooney* shows Shirley as
a typical bobby-soxer. Actually, she seldom wore bobby sox, liked

to dance but not to jitterbug, admired Frank Sinatra's voice but failed to swoon, and used only a little "jive talk."

Miss Annie Rooney was the last film in which Shirley danced. Her studio preferred to develop her as a straight dramatic actress.

However, she wants to dance again, hopes to do a musical comedy in the future.

Shirley's first grown-up glamour stills were taken by the noted photographer, George Hurrell. Her maturity was heralded by a *Life* cover picture titled "Shirley Temple Grows Up," by a LOOK cover picture showing her with her first upswept hair do.

224

Shirley gained considerable radio experience during the year which elapsed between the filming of *Miss Annie Rooney* and her return to pictures as David Selznick's protégée. She starred in *Junior Miss*, was guest star on *Let Yourself Go*, with Milton Berle, above.

Shirley speculates on the future, which is slightly more complicated for her — education, engagement *and* stardom.

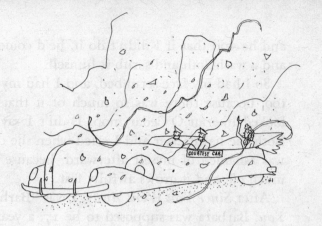

CHAPTER 10

Now and Tomorrow

When I was 15, I heard the big news that David O. Selznick wanted to sign a seven-year contract. Jiminy, I was thrilled! I have always thought he was "tops." I'd been crazy about *Rebecca* and *Gone with the Wind,* and about some of his stars—Vivien Leigh and Ingrid Bergman and Joan Fontaine. There wasn't anyone in Hollywood I'd have preferred to be with.

Mr. Selznick decided I should start in parts that were young and light, then let me grow into more romantic roles later on. I don't think I'll be cast to type the way I used to be, because he doesn't keep his stars in a rut. Another thing I like about him is that he's always willing to talk to me if I have any problems or ideas. He doesn't flatter me at all, but tells me straight out what I can do to improve. Also, he's a wonderful listener. He treats everything you say with the deepest sincerity, and then tells you whether or not you're right.

My first part with the Selznick Studio was as "Brig" in *Since You Went Away.* The part was fun, because Brig grew up quite a lot during the course of the picture. It gave me a chance to try to show, by little distinctions in my acting, how a girl's personality and mannerisms change in her early teens. In that part, Mr. Selznick made a great point of my not wearing any make-up at all. In fact, he insisted that I should actually scrub my face shiny,

227

and he said that if I didn't do it, he'd come to the set with soap and a washcloth and scrub it himself.

So I had my face scrubbed, and I had my hair cut and shaped, too, because there was so much of it that Mr. Selznick said it looked like an O'Cedar mop. Didn't I say he was no flatterer? Both the hairdresser and I cried when she cut my hair, though I was ashamed of myself afterward, because she didn't really cut much off, and it grows awfully fast.

After *Since You Went Away,* I was "Barbara" in *I'll Be Seeing You.* Barbara was supposed to be 17, a year older than I was at the time. *I'll Be Seeing You* was the first picture in which I ever made up for the camera, though I started using powder and lipstick for dates about the time most girls begin to. Mom brought me up on soap and water, taken externally. She thinks most girls have trouble with their skins because they don't keep them really clean, so I have always scrubbed and scrubbed, even in the pre-Selznick period.

Now I'm supposed to be back at the age of 15 again, for *Kiss and Tell,* which ought to be released just about the time I get to be a published author. It's funny how your age gets pushed around in movies, but, of course, clothes and make-up have a lot to do with how old any woman looks. *Kiss and Tell,* for which Mr. Selznick loaned me to Columbia studios is my most important part since I've grown up.

My school rules while making a picture were the same as they had always been — three hours of study a day, every weekday, before 4 o'clock. My teacher on *Kiss and Tell* was Mrs. Choate, supervised by Miss Barkley, who was my very first teacher when I started in movies. Each week Miss Barkley went to Westlake and got my assignments from the principal. At the end of the week she took my work to Westlake, where it was graded. She taught me everything but French. For that, a Westlake teacher came to the studio.

My French, incidentally, is peculiar. It seems that I have a dandy accent, but no vocabulary to match. When I went to Canada to take part in a War Loan Drive, various French dignitaries tried to speak French with me, because my accent made them think I really knew it. I was embarrassed because, though I could understand most of what they said, I just didn't have the words to answer them.

Keeping up with school work is not an easy thing while you're making a picture. This last year it was especially hectic, because I had the studio and school work and all the fuss that you go through when you're about to graduate, plus the excitement of getting myself engaged. Sometimes it seemed to me that actresses who had nothing to do but make movies were having a vacation. It's fortunate that I'm happiest when I have loads to do. On one of my pictures, an actress who was in most of my scenes used to go and lie down in her dressing room, with cold cloths on her eyes, whenever she finished a scene, and if anyone made any noise near her, it was just too bad. Meanwhile, I'd finish my scene and go off to write a paper on medieval art or an English theme about the connection between Ralph Waldo Emerson and the English romantic poets.

Here's the way a typical day went when I was making a picture. Let's pretend it was a year ago when I was going to school too. I roll out of bed before seven, to be at the studio by 8:30. Yes, 8:30! Mom and I have an argument about whether I should wear slacks or a dress to work. I win and wear slacks. We drive to the studio in the station wagon, and Mom listens to me say my lines on the way. (Fortunately, I'm a quick study. I can't understand people who walk up and down for hours muttering their lines to themselves. I get mine firmly in mind, and then ignore them. When the scene starts, I just relax, and when my cue comes, the lines just bubble out of me.)

Then, at the studio, I go to my dressing room, put on my clothes for the picture, and get a going-over from the make-up man. Next I go to the set. There's an argument about my hair, and they try it half a dozen ways. Braids, no braids. Ribbons, no ribbons. Pompadour, no pompadour. Everyone talks it all over, and finally they decide on braids, which make me look as if I ought to be sucking a lollipop, and I start acting. My nose always itches just after the director says, "Roll it."

You can easily play the same scene 10 or 12 times, not even counting rehearsals. First they make a master shot, with the camera looking at the scene as a whole. Then they change camera and

229

make lots of close-ups from various angles. Maybe in the middle of a take the telephone on the set rings, because somebody forgot to shut it off, and the sound track is ruined. Maybe an airplane goes overhead, or visitors on the set start talking. Or there's a shadow somewhere, or somebody blows his lines. In any case, it all has to be done over again.

When the director says, "Okay, print it," I'm through for a while, until they shift things around for the next take. I go to my dressing room and get to work writing a paper on Sam Houston, for my history class. Until lunch time, I go back and forth from Sam Houston to the camera. Finally it's 12 o'clock, and I begin counting minutes until the "window" shot is taken. We call it "window" because it's a little joke meaning "when do we eat?" In other words, it's lunch time. I'm starved because I only drink orange juice for breakfast.

I change back to my slacks, leaving my make-up on, and Mom and I drive over to the Brown Derby for lunch. We go there nearly every day, because only an hour is allowed for lunch, and they know we're coming and serve us in a hurry. We drive up to the side entrance, because in front there are always autograph hunters and people with cameras who want snapshots. Sometimes there's a guest with us, but I'm happier if there isn't, because at lunch I like to rest my mind on a "pillow."

A few weeks ago, I had quite an embarrassing experience while we were having lunch at the Brown Derby. I'd been out driving with a bunch of kids the Sunday before, and we were feeling peppy. Every time we saw a big, flashy car with a chauffeur, we'd lean out of the windows of the Ford we were in and yell, "Movie star, movie star!" Next week at lunch a man I didn't know came by and looked at me and said under his breath, "Movie star, movie star." Then he laughed. He was one of the people we'd yelled at, who, of course, we never expected to see again. He then introduced himself as the driver we had yelled at. Was my face red!

After lunch I go to my dressing room for a minute to catch my breath before returning to the set. Sometimes I get in a little studying, or telephone one of my girl friends to discuss plans for a party next Saturday night.

230

Afternoon is just like morning, with acting and studying mixed up together, except that for some reason there always seem to be more decisions to make in the afternoon. Maybe there's a debate about what I'm to wear for sports clothes in the picture. The wardrobe lady, the cameramen, Mom, a couple of publicity people, the fitter, director and Anita Colby, who is Mr. Selznick's stylist, all stand around discussing what kind of shorts I ought to wear. I try on the shorts, and they're horrid. Well, I had suspected all along that this would happen, and that's why I insisted on wearing slacks to work this morning, even if Mom didn't think they were quite ladylike.

So I put on my own slacks and they are fine. Then I discover some chocolate on them, and am very perturbed. But the director is delighted. He says, "Oh, a little chocolate will be just fine, it'll be all the more natural."

We decide on slacks. Then they wonder whether I shouldn't wear a midriff blouse with the slacks, and there's another long discussion about whether the Hays office will allow it. The Hays office, by the way, once killed a baby picture of me without any clothes on. You know, the pictures parents always take of a poor, defenseless baby lying on its stomach without a stitch of clothes. The Hays office said it suggested nudity, which was an understatement.

Anyhow, everyone concedes the midriff blouse and I play the scene that way. Then I go back to studying, and just as I am well under way again on Sam Houston, someone from the publicity department comes around about a picture of me that a film magazine wants for a June issue. They want the picture in cap and gown, and it doesn't do a bit of good to explain that Westlake girls graduate in long, plain white dresses. After 15 minutes' discussion, they still want the cap and gown. Okay, cap and gown. Then there is more discussion about a white cap and gown versus a black cap and gown. While everybody talks it over, I cast a vote for white and go back to Sam Houston.

At 5:30 the director calls quits, but work isn't over yet. Before I even change my clothes, we go to see the rushes, the scenes which were shot the day before. We sit in a tiny projection room and I watch myself on the screen, which has always bored me horribly except that it's a good way to check up on myself and see if I can improve. Then I change back to the controversial slacks and Mom and I go home.

Nearly always Mom and Daddy and I have dinner together. George eats with us if he's in town; Jack is married now, so even if he's in Hollywood on leave, he eats at home with his wife, except when they both come over. They have a darling baby, named Stanley, whom they usually bring over to see us on Sunday.

After dinner, if it was a school night, I'd settle down and study. I had more homework than my classmates, because they got two study periods during school hours. I studied with the radio on and had a few phone conversations with my friends. Then I went to bed.

When I'm not making pictures I can go out both Friday and Saturday, but since film people work on Saturdays, Friday is just like any other night if I'm doing a picture. Generally I either go dancing at the Cocoanut Grove or go to a party at somebody's house. Before I became engaged, I went out with a lot of different boys, every one of whom got a careful once-over from Mom and Daddy. Mom is always waiting for me when I get home, and I tell her all about it. Sometimes I have very amusing things to tell her, like people coming up to me in the Cocoanut Grove and saying, "Did anybody ever tell you that you look just like Shirley Temple?"

Sunday afternoon I play with my brother's baby, and usually some boys and girls come over, and we sit around drinking cokes, or go for a walk, or swim, or play badminton. Mostly we use the playhouse. That's my own special place, a little house of my own out in our yard. It has a room big enough to dance in, so that we won't wear out the floor of the big house, and a powder room for my girl friends, and a mirror-panelled soda fountain. It has a lower floor where we keep my collection of dolls, and all the costumes I've worn in my different pictures. There's a miniature stage, too, where we can show motion pictures.

We don't show Shirley Temple pictures, though, unless people actually insist upon them. My own films don't interest me one bit after I've made them. But I love other movies just as much as other youngsters my age. Being in films hasn't dulled my reaction

232

to them one bit.

I hope no one is going to be shocked when I say that I get the biggest bang out of horror pictures. If they're scary, you have fun being scared, and if they're not scary, they're so funny you can have a good time just laughing at them. Perhaps I feel that way partly because I have never had nightmares. Maybe being in movies has released my imagination, so that I don't have enough left to scare myself with. The only pictures that have ever haunted me after I saw them were *Night Must Fall* and *The Uninvited*.

Mary Lou Isleib and I saw *Night Must Fall* together, one New Year's Eve at our home when we were about 13. She had come to my house to spend the night. After the show, we got into the twin beds in my room and lay there scared to death. If I'd been alone, I don't think it would have bothered me, but Mary Lou and I scared each other, and we didn't dare go to sleep until we heard the family come upstairs.

The Uninvited was quite an experience, too. That's the picture where the ghost is heralded by the smell of mimosa. I saw it with a boy, on a very rainy night. When we got into the car afterwards, I could actually smell mimosa. After we got home we were still in a spooky mood, so we dug up a ouija board from somewhere. We didn't have it balanced on our knees just right, so it fell down, with a clatter. We both jumped so hard that we hit our heads together and nearly knocked ourselves out.

It's a good thing I've been so busy, because the last few years haven't been any dream of joy for anyone. Both my brothers were in the armed forces when war came. Jack was a staff sergeant with an Army Air Forces motion-picture unit, and George was a master technical sergeant in the Marines. He was at Pearl Harbor when it was bombed.

No one expected Pearl Harbor, of course. As it happened, we weren't even listening to the radio that Sunday. We were down at the pool. Bob, one of my friends, came over to the house and said, "Did you hear the news? Pearl Harbor's been bombed."

It was so terrible, not knowing whether George was alive or dead. I was going to be the staunch one, and I kept from crying for about half an hour, but then I had to give in. Mom was pretty upset too, and finally after a month had passed we didn't see how we could stand it any longer, so Daddy sent a telegram to J. Edgar Hoover and he found out for us that George was safe. I guess he remembered about making me a G-man and figured we G-men have to stick together.

Two years later, when George returned home, we found out what had happened. He was in the thick of the bombing, but fortunately was not hurt.

I've seen so many boys go off to war, boys who didn't have a worry in the world a year or two ago. I keep thinking about a 19-year-old boy I saw in a San Francisco Hospital. He came from New York City. When I told him I would be in New York that fall, he asked me if I would go to the zoo, or maybe a night spot with him. I said I would. It was pretty rugged to play that scene though. He didn't know it, but he was dying.

Now that I've grown up, I realize every day how much making pictures has taught me, especially how to get along with people. For instance, *I'll Be Seeing You* taught me a great deal about what a soldier goes through in battle, and how he's likely to feel when he gets back. Now, when I meet returned servicemen, at the U.S.O. or the Hollywood Canteen or my friends' parties, I know much better how to talk to them.

For instance, at a party the other day I went into the kitchen for a glass of water and there was a Marine just sticking around by himself with his hands in his pockets. He had a Pacific service ribbon and combat stars and the Purple Heart on his uniform, so I didn't have the heart to ask him why he wasn't with the others playing records and dancing. We just talked, and I didn't mention the war. I got him talking about when he was a kid at school and what he wanted to do later on. After a while he said, "Gee, I feel wonderful. Let's go get a coke." I felt wonderful too.

Jack Agar, my fiancé, is a sergeant in the Army Air Forces, and pretty terrific.

I met Jack about two years ago, when he came to our swimming pool with some friends of mine. I didn't see much of him that day, as he had to leave quite soon, but somehow I was sure he'd be back.

Next time I met him was at a tea at Zasu Pitts' home next door to us, and afterwards we went out on a double date. At this time

I hadn't met his sister, Joyce, who is a year older than I am. When I did meet her, I liked her so much that I persuaded her to come to Westlake for her junior and senior years, which she did. Our families became very good friends. Often Mrs. Agar comes to the studio with Mom to spend the day.

A little while after I met him, Jack went into the Army. Then for a long time he wasn't around very much. He was in Texas for nine months, and in Oregon for seven months. Whenever he had a furlough, he came to see me, but for a long time he didn't get serious.

Then, along about last Christmas, things did get sort of serious, and we decided that some day we'd be engaged. The families knew about it, and liked the idea, but they wanted us to wait as long as possible, on account of the war and my tender years. When Jack gave me a ring, a gorgeous square-cut diamond, Mom wanted me to keep the engagement a secret.

Maybe I should have, but I just couldn't. The very day after I got the ring, my class at Westlake was having a luncheon and theater party. I was wearing the ring under my glove, and you should have heard those girls squeal when I took the glove off. Somehow, I wanted them to be first to know, so I told them all about it. When Mom reproached me for not keeping the engagement a secret, I tried to convince her that really it was a secret still, because nobody knew about it except my 42 best friends, but she couldn't see it that way.

Mom herself got married at 17, but she thinks that 19 or even 20 is young enough for me to take the big step, and maybe she's right. Meanwhile, I'm enjoying my engagement. Jack calls me "Red," incidentally. He's over 6 feet tall, and very handsome.

I've pretty well given up plans for college, though this decision is subject to change without notice, as they say on the bus schedules. But I'll go on studying on my own—French, Spanish, English literature and cooking.

I've been asked lots of questions about radio and the stage. Of course, I've already done quite a bit of radio work. The stage is a different matter.

When I spoke at the *Herald Tribune* Forum in 1944, I was nervous thinking about it. Then when I arrived on the platform and saw such a sea of friendly faces in the audience, I felt reassured and got through my speech just fine. It was over before I really had a chance to worry about it.

That's about all I can say about my plans now. Jack isn't the least bit jealous of my work, and I don't see why I can't have a happy home and a family and make pictures too. Mr. Selznick thinks so. Pictures have been a part of my life for so long that it would be pretty hard for me to get along without them. Whenever I'm off the screen for a few months, I'm perfectly happy, but then a kind of urge comes over me, and I long to be back on a studio set again. So I'll go on making pictures as long as people want to see me on the screen.

Growing up in the midst of depression, recovery and world war, I was too young always to appreciate the significance of the times, but I hope now the fantasy of my early films gave audiences momentary escape from that troubled and eventful decade.

It has been fun writing this book. Looking back, I realize all over again that I've been a very lucky, very happy girl. If I've given pleasure to audiences, maybe it's kind of a return for the pleasure being on the screen has given me.

Shirley gets tossed around a bit at a pool party for servicemen, given by Joan Crawford and her husband, Philip Terry.

After swimming in the Terry pool, guests roared with laughter at a private showing, not of a film starring Joan or Shirley, but of Betty Grable in *Pin-up Girl*. Five-year-old Christina Terry,

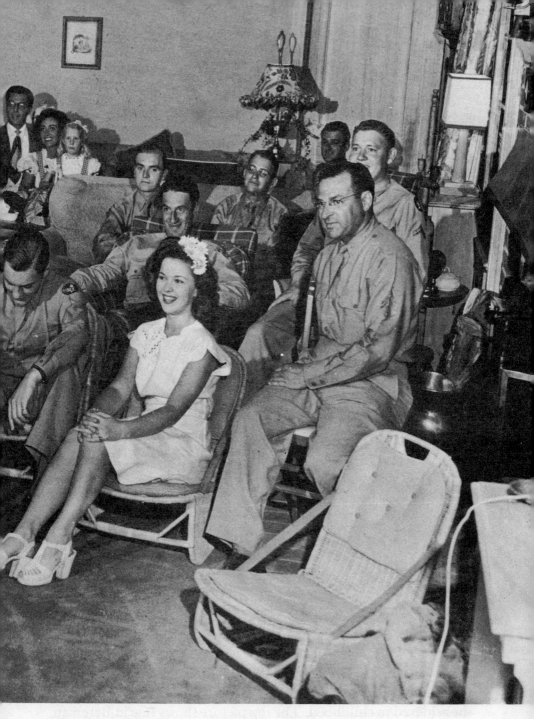

who appears in the background with her parents, enjoyed the party as much as the GI's. Later, Shirley did her best to dance with each and every one of the 20 soldiers.

Shirley's contract with David Selznick has five more years to run, and he well may guide her to stardom as brilliant as that which she achieved in childhood. The top picture shows Ingrid Bergman, left, and Jennifer Jones, right, who are also Selznick players. Miss Jones played with Shirley in *Since You Went Away,* a Selznick success.

Shirley's contract entitles her to two yearly vacations of three consecutive weeks each, permits her to go to college, to marry, and to have children. Realizing that a large part of Shirley's appeal is her wholesomeness and normality, Selznick wants her to lead the life of any other young girl, to remain unspoiled by stardom.

In *Since You Went Away*, Shirley played "Brig," typical American girl whose "crush" on Joseph Cotten, her older sister's sweetheart, greatly embarrasses him. She wore no make-up, not even powder.

In *I'll Be Seeing You*, Shirley played "Barbara," who nearly broke up the romance of her cousin, played by Ginger Rogers, by giving away the fact that the cousin was on temporary parole from jail.

Westlake School, where Shirley prepared for college. Although her school days are probably over, she plans to study on her own.

Shirley mixes a malted for herself at the soft-drink bar, feature of the "house" built for her on the grounds of the Temple home.

Shirley with her classmates during graduation exercises at Westlake School last June. In school, she was just "one of the girls."

Shirley helps two of her classmates, Nancy and Marion Majors, carry a heavy Mexican saddle down to the stables. They wear traditional blue jeans and moccasins instead of formal riding habits and boots.

The Temples enjoy family gatherings. Here Shirley lunches
with her sister-in-law, Mrs. Jack Temple, and her father.

Shirley's sixteenth birthday was celebrated with a party on the
set of *I'll Be Seeing You,* then in production. At Shirley's right
is Mary Lou Isleib, who again served as her stand-in for the
picture.

Before her engagement, Shirley was besieged with requests for dates. Left to right, she attends a Hollywood première with Seaman David Archer; dances with Shipfitter Buddy Culver at the U.S.O.; and rhumbas at the Stork Club with Lt. Barney Straus.

At the U.S.O. and the Hollywood Canteen, above, she is among the most popular of the hostesses. When fan writers asked whether any of her romances were serious, Shirley enjoyed parrying with a demure, "Yes, indeed, I'm very much interested in seven or eight boys."

Letters to servicemen come second only to school work on the list of Shirley's home duties. She gets over 3,000 letters a week from boys in the armed forces, once received a request from a four-star general for a picture to keep up the morale of his troops.

Left, Shirley speaks at the *Herald Tribune* Forum in New York. Right, she receives an award from Bob Hope as "the screen's most promising newcomer" at the LOOK Magazine Awards Dinner in Hollywood.

Batteries of photographers haunt Shirley whenever she goes dancing. At the Hollywood Palladium, Nacio Brown, Jr., one of Shirley's pre-engagement boy friends, found their attention highly "exasperating."

Jack Agar, 24 years old, whom Shirley describes blissfully as "over 6 feet tall and very handsome," won out over his legion of competitors. Their engagement was announced in the spring of 1945.

These youngsters, waiting patiently for Shirley to come out of
her New York hotel, are among the growing army of Temple
fans who some day may outnumber even the legions who loved
Shirley as a child star. David Selznick says, "I think that part
of Shirley Temple's great appeal is based on the fact that she has
grown up with a whole generation of moviegoers. The boys

and girls of America adored her when she was 4, when she was 8, and when she was 16. They still adore her, and, hopefully, she will continue to be their ideal representative on the screen. Moreover, she represents in personality and appearance, more than any other person on the screen, the best ideals of young America."

PICTURE CREDITS

PAGE	SOURCE	PAGE	SOURCE
142	top, Wide World; bottom, Keystone View	197	Culver Service
143	top left, Twentieth Century-Fox; top right, Doc Bishop; bottom, Underwood & Underwood	198	Twentieth Century-Fox
		199	Gene Kornman, Twentieth Century-Fox
144	Twentieth Century-Fox	200-201	Twentieth Century-Fox
145	Twentieth Century-Fox	202	Twentieth Century-Fox
146	top, Twentieth Century-Fox; bottom, Doc Bishop	203	Twentieth Century-Fox
		204-205	Twentieth Century-Fox
147	Twentieth Century-Fox	206	International News
148	Twentieth Century-Fox	213	left, Penguin Photo; right, International News
149	Twentieth Century-Fox		
150-151	Doc Bishop	214-215	Acme Newspictures
152	Twentieth Century-Fox	216	Wide World
161	Anthony Ugrin	217	Metro-Goldwyn-Mayer
162-163	Twentieth Century-Fox	218	John Engstead, LOOK
164	International News	219	Press Association
165	International News	220	Edward Small
166	top left, Twentieth Century-Fox; top right, Wide World; bottom, Twentieth Century-Fox	221	Edward Small
		222	Edward Small
		223	Edward Small
167	International News	224	George Hurrell
168	top, Earl Theisen, LOOK; bottom, Doc Bishop	225	Blue Network
		226	Selznick International
169	top, Twentieth Century-Fox; bottom, International News	237	Sprague Talbott, International News
		238-239	Sprague Talbott, International News
170	International News	240	Earl Theisen, LOOK
171	Shirley Temple	241	Earl Theisen, LOOK
172	Shirley Temple	242	Selznick International
173	Shirley Temple	243	Selznick International
174	Shirley Temple	244	Selznick International
175	Shirley Temple	245	Acme Newspictures
176	Twentieth Century-Fox	246	Selznick International
185	Twentieth Century-Fox	247	top, Wide World; bottom, Selznick International
186	Twentieth Century-Fox	248	top left, International News; top center, Wide World; top right, Stork Club; bottom, Wide World
187	Twentieth Century-Fox		
188	Twentieth Century-Fox		
189	Twentieth Century-Fox	249	Earl Theisen, LOOK
190	Twentieth Century-Fox	250	top left, International News; top right, Selznick International; bottom, Wide World
191	Twentieth Century-Fox		
192	Twentieth Century-Fox		
193	Twentieth Century-Fox	251	Press Association
194	Twentieth Century-Fox	252-253	International News; By-Line
195	Twentieth Century-Fox		
196	Twentieth Century-Fox		

The editors of LOOK Magazine wish to make special acknowledgments to Doc Bishop, Irving Cummings, Jim Denton, Gladys Drake, Hugh Harrison, Inez Hendricks, Frances Klampt, David O. Selznick, Arthur Treacher, Anthony Ugrin; also Jerry Pickman, Henry Klinger and Films Incorporated and Fox Movietone News for their help in assembling picture material for this book.